# Touchstones

A TEACHING ANTHOLOGY
Revised and expanded edition

MICHAEL AND PETER BENTON

Hodder & Stoughton
LONDON SYDNEY AUCKLAND

# Illustration Acknowledgments

The editors and publishers would also like to thank the following for permission to reproduce illustrations:

National Portrait Gallery, London: 'Sir Walter Raleigh' by Nicholas Hilliard (p. 8); National Gallery of Art, Washington DC, Samuel H. Cress Collection: 'Death and the Miser' by Bosch (p. 16); The Mansell Collection: 'Knight, Death and the Devil' by Dürer (p. 21); National Gallery of Art, Washington DC, Rosenwald Collection: 'The Cry' by Edward Munch (p. 23); Mrs Carol Ann Danes/Needham & Grant: 'Woman with a Handbag' by L. S. Lowry (p. 30); Clichés Musées Nationaux: 'The Circus' by Seurat (p. 33); and 'Approach to the Village' by Pissarro (pp. 50–1); Bill Brandt: 'Portrait of a Young Girl, Eaton Place' (p. 34); Salford Art Gallery & Museum: 'St Stephen's Church, Salford' by L. S. Lowry (p. 44); John Topham Ltd and the *Guardian*: 'Aerial Patterns at Harvest Time' (p. 53); Oslo Kommunes Künstsamlinger, Munch-Museet: 'Attraction' by Edward Munch (p. 58); The Mansell Collection: 'Dancer with a bouquet' by Degas (p. 66); Imperial War Museum: 'A Dead German Outside his Dugout, Beaumont-Hamel, November, 1916' (p. 77) and First World War recruiting posters (pp. 80–1); The Tate Gallery: 'La Mitrailleuse' by C. R. W. Nevinson (p. 82); Camera Press (p. 87); Henry Moore: 'Atom Piece' (p. 93) and 'Rocking Chair No. 2' (p. 137); The John Hillelson Agency Ltd: 'Three Priests' (p. 103), 'Girl with a Doll, Washington' (p. 117); 'Beirut' (p. 121); 'Butchers at Work' (p. 180); 'The End is at Hand' (p. 186); 'Confrontation: Pentagon, Washington' (pp. 112–13); Philip Jones Griffiths and the *Guardian*: 'Youth Against the Bomb' (pp. 128–9); The British Museum: Cartoon by Bruno Paul (p. 134); Fernand Leger Museum and SPADEM, Paris: 'The Builders' by Leger (p. 152); Tony Stone Ltd (p. 171); Edward S. Ross (p. 199); Patrimoine des Musées Royaux des Beaux-Arts, Brussels: 'The Fall of Icarus' by Brueghel (pp. 204–5).

First published 1968
Second edition 1970
Third edition 1988
Fifth impression 1992

ISBN 0 340 40820 0

Typeset by Rowland Phototypesetting Ltd, Bury St Edmunds, Suffolk.
Printed in Great Britain for the educational publishing division of Hodder & Stoughton Ltd, Mill Road, Dunton Green, Sevenoaks, Kent by St Edmundsbury Press Ltd, Bury St Edmunds, Suffolk.

# Contents

# Days

## Days

What are days for?
Days are where we live.
They come, they wake us
Time and time over.
They are to be happy in:
Where can we live but days?
Ah, solving that question
Brings the priest and the doctor
In their long coats
Running over the fields.

PHILIP LARKIN

## What is our Life?

What is our life? A play of passion.
And what our mirth but music of division?
Our mothers' wombs the tiring houses be
Where we are dressed for this short comedy.
Heaven the judicious sharp spectator is
Who sits and marks what here we do amiss.
The graves that hide us from the searching sun
Are like drawn curtains when the play is done.
Thus playing post we to our latest rest,
And then we die in earnest, not in jest.

SIR WALTER RALEIGH

# The Lie

Go, soul, the body's guest,
  Upon a thankless arrant;
Fear not to touch the best;
  The truth shall be thy warrant.
    Go, since I needs must die,
    And give the world the lie.

Say to the court, it glows
  And shines like rotten wood;
Say to the church, it shows
  What's good, and doth no good:
    If church and court reply,
    Then give them both the lie.

Tell potentates, they live
  Acting by other's action,
Not loved unless they give,
  Not strong but by affection:
    If potentates reply,
    Give potentates the lie.

Tell men of high condition
    That manage the estate,
Their purpose is ambition,
    Their practice only hate:
        And if they once reply,
        Then give them all the lie.

Tell them that brave it most,
    They beg for more by spending,
Who, in their greatest cost,
    Seek nothing but commending:
        And if they make reply,
        Then give them all the lie.

Tell zeal it wants devotion;
    Tell love it is but lust;
Tell time it metes but motion;
    Tell flesh it is but dust:
        And wish them not reply,
        For thou must give the lie.

Tell age it daily wasteth;
    Tell honour how it alters;
Tell beauty how she blasteth;
    Tell favour how it falters:
        And as they shall reply,
        Give every one the lie.

Tell wit how much it wrangles
    In tickle points of niceness;
Tell wisdom she entangles
    Herself in over-wiseness:
        And when they do reply,
        Straight give them both the lie.

Tell physic of her boldness;
    Tell skill it is prevention;
Tell charity of coldness;
    Tell law it is contention:
        And as they do reply,
        So give them still the lie.

Tell fortune of her blindness;
 Tell nature of decay;
Tell friendship of unkindness;
 Tell justice of delay:
  And if they will reply,
  Then give them all the lie.

Tell arts they have no soundness,
 But vary by esteeming;
Tell schools they want profoundness,
 And stand too much on seeming:
  If arts and schools reply,
  Give arts and schools the lie.

Tell faith it's fled the city;
 Tell how the country erreth;
Tell, manhood shakes off pity;
 Tell, virtue least preferreth:
  And if they do reply,
  Spare not to give the lie.

So when thou hast, as I
 Commanded thee, done blabbing,
Although to give the lie
 Deserves no less than stabbing,
  Stab at thee he that will,
  No stab thy soul can kill.

SIR WALTER RALEIGH

# One Evening

As I walked out one evening,
 Walking down Bristol Street,
The crowds upon the pavement
 Were fields of harvest wheat.

And down by the brimming river
 I heard a lover sing
Under an arch of the railway:
 'Love has no ending.

I'll love you, dear, I'll love you
    Till China and Africa meet,
And the river jumps over the mountain
    And the salmon sing in the street.

I'll love you till the ocean
    Is folded and hung up to dry,
And the seven stars go squawking
    Like geese about the sky.

The years shall run like rabbits,
    For in my arms I hold
The Flower of the Ages,
    And the first love of the world.'

But all the clocks in the city
    Began to whirr and chime:
'O let not Time deceive you,
    You cannot conquer Time.

'In the burrows of the Nightmare
    Where Justice naked is,
Time watches from the shadow
    And coughs when you would kiss.

'In headaches and in worry
    Vaguely life leaks away,
And Time will have his fancy
    To-morrow or to-day.

'Into many a green valley
    Drifts the appalling snow;
Time breaks the threaded dances
    And the diver's brilliant bow.

'O plunge your hands in water,
    Plunge them in up to the wrist;
Stare, stare in the basin
    And wonder what you've missed.

'The glacier knocks in the cupboard,
    The desert sighs in the bed,

And the crack in the tea-cup opens
   A lane to the land of the dead.

'Where the beggars raffle the banknotes
   And the Giant is enchanting to Jack,
And the Lily-white Boy is a Roarer,
   And Jill goes down on her back.

'O look, look in the mirror,
   O look in your distress;
Life remains a blessing
   Although you cannot bless.

'O stand, stand at the window
   As the tears scald and start;
You shall love your crooked neighbour
   With your crooked heart'.

It was late, late in the evening
   The lovers they were gone;
The clocks had ceased their chiming,
   And the deep river ran on.

W. H. AUDEN

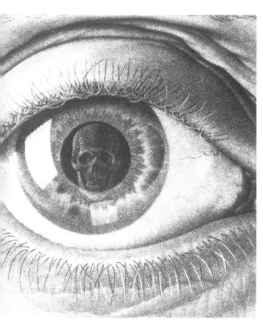

## 'I Look Into My Glass'

I look into my glass,
And view my wasting skin,
And say, 'Would God it came to pass
My heart had shrunk as thin!'

For then, I, undistrest
By hearts grown cold to me,
Could lonely wait my endless rest
With equanimity.

But Time, to make me grieve,
Part steals, lets part abide;
And shakes this fragile frame at eve
With throbbings of noontide.

THOMAS HARDY

# Death on a Live Wire

Treading a field I saw afar
A laughing fellow climbing the cage
That held the grinning tensions of wire,
Alone, and no girl gave him courage.

Up he climbed on the diamond struts,
Diamond cut diamond, till he stood
With the insulators brooding like owls
And all their live wisdom if he would.

I called to him climbing and asked him to say
What thrust him into the singeing sky:
The one word he told me the wind took away,
So I shouted again, but the wind passed me by

And the gust of his answer tore at his coat
And stuck him stark on the lightning's bough;
Humanity screeched in his manacled throat
And he cracked with flame like a figure of straw.

Turning, burning, he dangled black,
A hot sun swallowing at his fork
And shaking embers out of his back,
Planting his shadow of fear in the chalk.

O then he danced an incredible dance
With soot in his sockets, hanging at heels;
Uprooted mandrakes screamed in his loins,
His legs thrashed and lashed like electric eels;

For now he embraced the talent of iron,
The white-hot ore that comes from the hill,
The Word out of which the electrons run,
The snake in the rod and the miracle;

And as he embraced it the girders turned black,
Fused metal wept and great tears ran down
Till his fingers like snails at last came unstuck
And he fell through the cage of the sun.

MICHAEL BALDWIN

# 'Out, Out—'

The buzz saw snarled and rattled in the yard
And made dust and dropped stove-length sticks of wood,
Sweet-scented stuff when the breeze drew across it.
And from there those that lifted eyes could count
Five mountain ranges one behind the other
Under the sunset far into Vermont.
And the saw snarled and rattled, snarled and rattled,
As it ran light, or had to bear a load.
And nothing happened: day was all but done.
Call it a day, I wish they might have said
To please the boy by giving him the half hour
That a boy counts so much when saved from work.
His sister stood beside them in her apron
To tell them 'Supper'. At the word, the saw,
As if to prove saws knew what supper meant,
Leaped out at the boy's hand, or seemed to leap—
He must have given the hand. However it was,
Neither refused the meeting. But the hand!
The boy's first outcry was a rueful laugh,
As he swung toward them holding up the hand
Half in appeal, but half as if to keep
The life from spilling. Then the boy saw all—
Since he was old enough to know, big boy
Doing a man's work, though a child at heart—
He saw all spoiled. 'Don't let him cut my hand off—
The doctor, when he comes. Don't let him sister!'
So. But the hand was gone already.
The doctor put him in the dark of ether.
He lay and puffed his lips out with his breath.
And then—the watcher at his pulse took fright.
No one believed. They listened at his heart.
Little—less—nothing!—and that ended it.
No more to build on there. And they, since they
Were not the one dead, turned to their affairs.

ROBERT FROST

# Mid-Term Break

I sat all morning in the college sick bay
Counting bells knelling classes to a close.
At two o'clock our neighbours drove me home.

In the porch I met my father crying—
He had always taken funerals in his stride—
And Big Jim Evans saying it was a hard blow.

The baby cooed and laughed and rocked the pram
When I came in, and I was embarrassed
By old men standing up to shake my hand

And tell me they were 'sorry for my trouble',
Whispers informed strangers I was the eldest,
Away at school, as my mother held my hand

In hers and coughed out angry tearless sighs.
At ten o'clock the ambulance arrived
With the corpse, stanched and bandaged by the nurses.

Next morning I went up into the room. Snowdrops
And candles soothed the bedside; I saw him
For the first time in six weeks. Paler now,

Wearing a poppy bruise on his left temple,
He lay in the four foot box as in his cot.
No gaudy scars, the bumper knocked him clear.

A four foot box, a foot for every year.

SEAMUS HEANEY

# At The Florist's

A man enters a florist's
and chooses some flowers
the florist wraps up the flowers
the man puts his hand in his pocket
to find the money
the money to pay for the flowers
but at the same time he puts
all of a sudden
his hand on his heart
and he falls

At the same time that he falls
the money rolls on the floor
and then the flowers fall
at the same time as the man
at the same time as the money
and the florist stands there
with the money rolling
with the flowers spoiling
with the man dying
obviously this is very sad
and she's got to do something
the florist
but she doesn't know quite where to start
she doesn't know
at which end to begin

There's so many things to do
with this man dying
with these flowers spoiling
and this money
this money that rolls
that doesn't stop rolling.

JACQUES PRÉVERT
*(trans. L. Ferlinghetti)*

# Do Not Go Gentle Into That Good Night

Do not go gentle into that good night,
Old age should burn and rave at close of day;
Rage, rage against the dying of the light.

Though wise men at their end know dark is right,
Because their words had forked no lightning they
Do not go gentle into that good night.

Good men, the last wave by, crying how bright
Their frail deeds might have danced in a green bay,
Rage, rage against the dying of the light.

Wild men who caught and sang the sun in flight,
And learn, too late, they grieved it on its way,
Do not go gentle into that good night.

Grave men, near death, who see with blinding sight
Blind eyes could blaze like meteors and be gay,
Rage, rage against the dying of the light.

And you, my father, there on the sad height,
Curse, bless, me now with your fierce tears, I pray.
Do not go gentle into that good night.
Rage, rage against the dying of the light.

DYLAN THOMAS

# Because I Could Not Stop for Death

Because I could not stop for Death—
He kindly stopped for me—
The Carriage held but just Ourselves—
And Immortality.

We slowly drove—He knew no haste
And I had put away
My labor and my leisure too,
For His Civility—

We passed the School, where Children strove
At Recess—in the Ring—
We passed the Fields of Gazing Grain—
We passed the Setting Sun—

Or rather—He passed Us—
The Dews drew quivering and chill—
For only Gossamer, my Gown—
My Tippet—only Tulle—

We paused before a House that seemed
A Swelling of the Ground—
A Roof was scarcely visible—
The Cornice—in the Ground—

Since then—'tis Centuries—and yet
Feels shorter than the Day
I first surmised the Horses' Heads
Were toward Eternity—

EMILY DICKINSON

# Death Be Not Proud

Death be not proud, though some have called thee
Mighty and dreadful, for, thou art not soe,
For, those, whom thou think'st, thou dost overthrow,
Die not, poore death, nor yet canst thou kill mee;
From rest and sleepe, which but thy pictures bee,
Much pleasure, then from thee, much more must flow,
And soonest our best men with thee doe goe,
Rest of their bones, and soules deliverie.
Thou art slave to Fate, chance, kings, and desperate men,
And dost with poyson, warre, and sicknesse dwell,
And poppie, or charmes can make us sleepe as well,
And better than thy stroake; why swell'st thou then?
One short sleepe past, wee wake eternally,
And death shall be no more, Death thou shalt die.

JOHN DONNE

# Sonnet 71

No longer mourn for me when I am dead
Than you shall hear the surly sullen bell
Give warning to the world that I am fled
From this vile world, with vilest worms to dwell:
Nay, if you read this line, remember not
The hand that writ it; for I love you so,
That I in your sweet thoughts would be forgot,
If thinking on me then should make you woe.
O, if, I say, you look upon this verse
When I perhaps compounded am with clay,
Do not so much as my poor name rehearse,
But let your love even with my life decay;
    Lest the wise world should look into your moan,
    And mock you with me after I am gone.

WILLIAM SHAKESPEARE

# 5 Ways to Kill a Man

There are many cumbersome ways to kill a man:
you can make him carry a plank of wood
to the top of a hill and nail him to it. To do this
properly you require a crowd of people
wearing sandals, a cock that crows, a cloak
to dissect, a sponge, some vinegar and one
man to hammer the nails home.

Or you can take a length of steel,
shaped and chased in a traditional way,
and attempt to pierce the metal cage he wears.
But for this you need white horses,
English trees, men with bows and arrows,
at least two flags, a prince and a
castle to hold your banquet in.

Dispensing with nobility, you may, if the wind
allows, blow gas at him. But then you need
a mile of mud sliced through with ditches,
not to mention black boots, bomb craters,
more mud, a plague of rats, a dozen songs
and some round hats made of steel.

In an age of aeroplanes, you may fly
miles above your victim and dispose of him by
pressing one small switch. All you then
require is an ocean to separate you, two
systems of government, a nation's scientists,
several factories, a psychopath and
land that no one needs for several years.

These are, as I began, cumbersome ways
to kill a man. Simpler, direct, and much more neat
is to see that he is living somewhere in the middle
of the twentieth century, and leave him there.

EDWIN BROCK

★ **Talking and Writing.** Several of the poems in this section ask and attempt to answer the question posed by Sir Walter Raleigh, *What is our Life?* If life has a purpose, whose purpose is it and what might it be? Raleigh, four hundred years ago, compared our brief existence to a performance on a stage. What might be appropriate images for life in the last years of the twentieth century—a motorway journey, a flight, a film, a TV soap opera? Look carefully at the images in Raleigh's poem ('tiring houses' means dressing rooms—where actors put on their attire—by the way) and if you have an idea for a modern *What is our Life?* try to develop it into a poem of your own beginning with the same words.

—The title poem to this section, Philip Larkin's *Days* on page 7 asks the question 'What are days for?' and answers it indirectly. Discuss the poem in pairs and decide what you think is the main idea the poem expresses.

—What *are* days for? Try to write a seventeen-syllable haiku (five syllables on the first line, seven on the second and five on the third) which concentrates on capturing in *a single image* your answer to this question.

★ **Performance.** Walter Raleigh wrote his poem *The Lie* when imprisoned in the Tower. He was executed in 1618. It is a powerful piece which seems to proclaim the man's honesty and fearlessness. In groups, decide how the poem might best be given a dramatic reading using several voices, rehearse it and present it to the rest of the class either as a live performance or as a tape recording.

—W. H. Auden's poem *One Evening* on page 10 seems made for performance. There is the voice of the Narrator, the voice of the Lover, the voice of Time. In groups, after listening to the poem being read, discuss the images and the ideas that the poem suggests to you. Still in your groups, divide the poem up and present a recorded or live performance. If you want to use more than three voices you can split the Lover's lines between two people and the verses spoken by Time can each be given a different voice.

★ **The Sixth Way.** On page 20 Edwin Brock suggests *5 Ways to Kill a Man.* Either write your own verse for the poem or try to create a parallel poem of your own—(Somebody wrote *5 ways to Annoy a Teacher*). It is a good poem to perform using four or five voices.

⋆ **Poems and Pictures.** If you or your parents have a photograph album, you will know that looking back at scenes from the past, although it can be very enjoyable, sometimes makes you stop and think. Did I really look like that? Is it really me? Is there any link between the baby in the picture and the me of today? Did my parents look and dress like that? Is my friend in the picture there at all like the friend who has grown up with me? If you have a chance to do so, look back over such a collection and try to record what you feel in a piece of your own.

# People And Places

## Ghost Stories

'Don't peep or the Bogey Man will get you!'
my great grandmother'd say as she held kids
under her shawl, but I looked in vain from
my mother's cardigan and no-one came.

At school, I told others ghost stories—
but could feel no frisson of fear myself—
James, Poe, Le Fanu, with added horrors.
'Have you heard the one' I'd start over lunch
'about the rotting nun?'

There were two odd handles in the front rooms
of our Victorian house. One was painted
pale grey like the Study's walls, the other—
brass-plated wearing thin. 'Some sort of bell
to call servants in the old days.'

When I was on my own I'd take a breath
and slowly move one of the handles up,
imagine *them*, turning the knob softly,
opening the door and coming in.

I'd visualise a pair—maid and butler
perhaps, in black going a little green,
their hair and eyebrows white, aged farcically
beyond old age, like the oldest members
of dynasties in epic film sagas.

Then, I'd put the handle back down again
and make them go away.

FIONA PITT-KETHLEY

# Poem in October

It was my thirtieth year to heaven
Woke to my hearing from harbour and neighbour wood
And the mussel pooled and the heron
Priested shore
The morning beckon
With water praying and call of seagull and rook
And the knock of sailing boats on the net webbed wall
Myself to set foot
That second
In the still sleeping town and set forth.

My birthday began with the water—
Birds and the birds of the winged trees flying my name
Above the farms and the white horses
And I rose
In rainy autumn
And walked abroad in a shower of all my days.
High tide and the heron dived when I took the road
Over the border
And the gates
Of the town closed as the town awoke.

A springful of larks in a rolling
Cloud and the roadside bushes brimming with whistling
Blackbirds and the sun of October
Summery
On the hill's shoulder,
Here were fond climates and sweet singers suddenly
Come in the morning where I wandered and listened
To the rain wringing
Wind blow cold
In the wood faraway under me.

Pale rain over the dwindling harbour
And over the sea wet church the size of a snail
With its horns through mist and the castle
Brown as owls
But all the gardens
Of spring and summer were blooming in the tall tales
Beyond the border and under the lark full cloud.

There could I marvel
   My birthday
Away but the weather turned around.


It turned away from the blithe country
And down the other air and the blue altered sky
   Streamed again a wonder of summer
      With apples
   Pears and red currants
And I saw in the turning so clearly a child's
Forgotten mornings when he walked with his mother
   Through the parables
      Of sun light
   And the legends of the green chapels


   And the twice told fields of infancy
That his tears burned my cheeks and his heart moved in mine.
   These were the woods the river and sea
      Where a boy
   In the listening
Summertime of the dead whispered the truth of his joy
To the trees and the stones and the fish in the tide.
   And the mystery
      Sang alive
   Still in the water and singingbirds.


   And there could I marvel my birthday
Away but the weather turned around. And the true
   Joy of the long dead child sang burning
      In the sun.
   It was my thirtieth
Year to heaven stood there then in the summer noon
Though the town below lay leaved with October blood.
   O may my heart's truth
      Still be sung
On this high hill in a year's turning.

DYLAN THOMAS

# Mr. Bleaney

'This was Mr. Bleaney's room. He stayed
The whole time he was at the Bodies, till
They moved him.' Flowered curtains, thin and frayed,
Fall to within five inches of the sill,

Whose window shows a strip of building land,
Tussocky, littered. 'Mr. Bleaney took
My bit of garden properly in hand.'
Bed, upright chair, sixty-watt bulb, no hook

Behind the door, no room for books or bags—
'I'll take it.' So it happens that I lie
Where Mr. Bleaney lay, and stub my fags
On the same saucer-souvenir, and try

Stuffing my ears with cotton-wool, to drown
The jabbering set he egged her on to buy.
I know his habits—what time he came down,
His preference for sauce to gravy, why

He kept on plugging at the four aways—
Likewise their yearly frame: the Frinton folk
Who put him up for summer holidays,
And Christmas at his sister's house in Stoke.

But if he stood and watched the frigid wind
Tousling the clouds, lay on the fusty bed
Telling himself that this was home, and grinned,
And shivered, without shaking off the dread

That how we live measures our own nature,
And at his age having no more to show
Than one hired box should make him pretty sure
He warranted no better, I don't know.

PHILIP LARKIN

# Mr Strugnell

'This was Mr Strugnell's room,' she'll say,
And look down at the lumpy, single bed.
'He stayed here up until he went away
And kept his bicycle out in that shed.

'He had a job at Norwood library—
He was a quiet sort who liked to read—
Dick Francis mostly, and some poetry—
He liked John Betjeman very much indeed

'But not Pam Ayres or even Patience Strong—
He'd change the subject if I mentioned them,
Or say "It's time for me to run along—
Your taste's too highbrow for me, Mrs M."

'And up he'd go and listen to that jazz.
I don't mind telling you it was a bore—
Few things in this house have been tiresome as
The sound of his foot tapping on the floor.

'He didn't seem the sort for being free
With girls or going out and having fun.
He had a funny turn in 'sixty-three
And ran round shouting "Yippee! It's begun."

'I don't know what he meant but after that
He had a different look, much more relaxed.
Some nights he'd come in late, too tired to chat,
As if he had been somewhat overtaxed.

'And now he's gone. He said he found Tulse Hill
Too stimulating—wanted somewhere dull.
At last he's found a place that fits the bill—
Enjoying perfect boredom up in Hull.'

WENDY COPE

# Daft Annie On Our Village Mainstreet

Annie
with your euphemisms to clothe you
with your not all there
        your sixpence short in the shilling
with your screw loose
        your crazy tick tock in the head
        your lurching pendulum
                                slightly unbalanced
with your plimsolls in winter
with your big-boots in summer and
        your own particular unseasonal
        your unpredictable weather.

Annie
out of the mainstream
mainstreet Annie
down at the Cross
with your religious mania
singing Salvation Army choruses
to all on Sunday.
Annie
with your unique place
        your pride of place
        in the community—
how
        to every village
        its doctor and its dominie
        its idiot.

Annie
with the village kids afraid of you
with your myth of witchery
with your mystery
        your big raw bones
and your hamfisted face.
with your touching every lamp-post
        your careful measured paces down mainstreet
clothed in euphemisms
and epithets.
Daft Annie
your epitaph.

LIZ LOCHHEAD

# The Clown III

Others are noble and admired—
The ones who walk the tightrope without nets,
The one who goes inside the lion's cage,
And all the grave, audacious acrobats.
Away from fear and rage
He simply is the interval for tired

People who cannot bear
Too much excitement. They can see in him
Their own lost innocence or else their fear
(For him no metal bars or broken limb).
Have they forgotten that it takes as much
Boldness to tumble, entertain and jest
When loneliness walks tightropes in your breast
And every joke is like a wild beast's touch?

ELIZABETH JENNINGS

# The Old Men Admiring Themselves in the Water

I heard the old, old men say,
'Everything alters,
And one by one we drop away.'
They had hands like claws, and their knees
Were twisted like the old thorn-trees
By the waters.
I heard the old, old men say,
'All that's beautiful drifts away
Like the waters.'

W. B. YEATS

# Not Waving But Drowning

Nobody heard him, the dead man,
But still he lay moaning:
I was much further out than you thought
And not waving but drowning.

Poor chap, he always loved larking
And now he's dead
It must have been too cold for him his heart gave way,
They said.

Oh, no no no no, it was too cold always
(Still the dead one lay moaning)
I was much too far out all my life
And not waving but drowning.

STEVIE SMITH

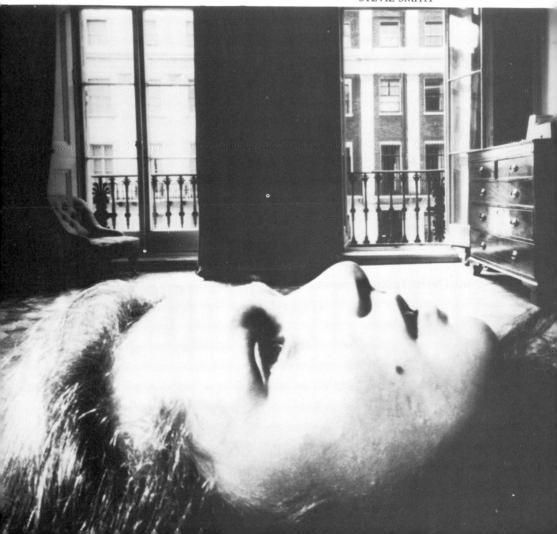

# Skanking Englishman Between Trains

(*Skanking = walking in reggae rhythm*)

Met him at Birmingham Station
small yellow hair Englishman
hi fi stereo swinging in one hand
walking in rhythm to reggae sound/Man

he was alive
he was full-o-jive
said he had a lovely
Jamaican wife

Said he couldn't remember
the taste of English food
I like mih drops
me johnny cakes
me peas and rice
me soup/Man

he was alive
he was full-o-jive
said he had a lovely
Jamaican wife

Said, showing me her photo
whenever we have a little quarrel
you know/to sweeten her up
I surprise her with a nice mango/Man

he was alive
he was full-o-jive
said he had a lovely Jamaican wife

GRACE NICHOLS

35

# Phenomenal Woman

Pretty women wonder where my secret lies.
I'm not cute or built to suit a fashion model's size
But when I start to tell them,
They think I'm telling lies.
I say,
It's in the reach of my arms,
The span of my hips,
The stride of my step,
The curl of my lips.
I'm a woman
Phenomenally.
Phenomenal woman,
That's me.

I walk into a room
Just as cool as you please,
And to a man,
The fellows stand or
Fall down on their knees.
Then they swarm around me,
A hive of honey bees.
I say,
It's the fire in my eyes,
And the flash of my teeth,
The swing in my waist,
And the joy in my feet.
I'm a woman
Phenomenally.
Phenomenal woman,
That's me.

Men themselves have wondered
What they see in me.
They try so much
But they can't touch
My inner mystery.
When I try to show them
They say they still can't see.
I say,
It's in the arch of my back,
The sun of my smile,
The ride of my breasts,
The grace of my style.
I'm a woman
Phenomenally.
Phenomenal woman,
That's me.

Now you understand
Just why my head's not bowed.
I don't shout or jump about
Or have to talk real loud.
When you see me passing
It ought to make you proud.
I say,
It's in the click of my heels,
The bend of my hair,
The palm of my hand,
The need for my care.
'Cause I'm a woman
Phenomenally.
Phenomenal woman,
That's me.

MAYA ANGELOU

# City Johannesburg

This way I salute you:
My hand pulses to my back trousers pocket
Or into my inner jacket pocket
For my pass,[1] my life,
Jo'burg City.[2]
My hand like a starved snake rears my pockets
For my thin, ever lean wallet,
While my stomach groans a friendly smile to hunger,
Jo'burg City.
My stomach also devours coppers and papers
Don't you know?
Jo'burg City, I salute you;
When I run out, or roar in a bus to you,
I leave behind me, my love,
My comic houses and people, my dongas[3] and my ever whirling
    dust,
My death,
That's so related to me as a wink to the eye.
Jo'burg City
I travel on your black and white and robotted[4] roads,
Through your thick iron breath that you inhale,
At six in the morning and exhale from five noon.
Jo'burg City
That is the time when I come to you,
When your neon flowers flaunt from your electrical wind,
That is the time when I leave you,
When your neon flowers flaunt their way through the falling
    darkness
On your cement trees.

[1] identity card
[2] abbreviation used with 'City' renders the endearment cynical
[3] hollows in ground, gouged by storm water
[4] traffic lights are referred to as robots in South Africa

And as I go back, to my love,
My dongas, my dust, my people, my death,
Where death lurks in the dark like a blade in the flesh,
I can feel your roots, anchoring your might, my feebleness
In my flesh, in my mind, in my blood,
And everything about you says it,
That, that is all you need of me.
Jo'burg City, Johannesburg,
Listen when I tell you,
There is no fun, nothing, in it.
When you leave the women and men with such frozen
    expressions,
Expressions that have tears like furrows of soil erosion,
Jo'burg City, you are like death,
Jo'burg City, Johannesburg, Jo'burg City.

MONGANE WALLY SEROTE

# The Whitsun Weddings

That Whitsun, I was late getting away:
    Not till about
One-twenty on the sunlit Saturday
Did my three-quarters-empty train pull out,
All windows down, all cushions hot, all sense
Of being in a hurry gone. We ran
Behind the backs of houses, crossed a street
Of blinding windscreens, smelt the fish-dock; thence
The river's level drifting breadth began,
Where sky and Lincolnshire and water meet.

All afternoon, through the tall heat that slept
    For miles inland,
A slow and stopping curve southwards we kept.
Wide farms went by, short-shadowed cattle, and
Canals with floatings of industrial froth;
A hothouse flashed uniquely: hedges dipped
And rose: and now and then a smell of grass
Displaced the reek of buttoned carriage-cloth
Until the next town, new and nondescript,
Approached with acres of dismantled cars.

At first, I didn't notice what a noise
    The weddings made
Each station that we stopped at: sun destroys
The interest of what's happening in the shade,
And down the long cool platforms whoops and skirls
I took for porters larking with the mails,
And went on reading. Once we started, though,
We passed them, grinning and pomaded, girls
In parodies of fashion, heels and veils,
All posed irresolutely, watching us go,

As if out on the end of an event
    Waving goodbye
To something that survived it. Struck, I leant
More promptly out next time, more curiously,
And saw it all again in different terms:
The fathers with broad belts under their suits
And seamy foreheads; mothers loud and fat;
An uncle shouting smut; and then the perms,
The nylon gloves and jewellery-substitutes,
The lemons, mauves, and olive-ochres that

Marked off the girls unreally from the rest.
    Yes, from cafés
And banquet-halls up yards, and bunting-dressed
Coach-party annexes, the wedding-days
Were coming to an end. All down the line
Fresh couples climbed aboard: the rest stood round;
The last confetti and advice were thrown,
And, as we moved, each face seemed to define

Just what it saw departing: children frowned
At something dull; fathers had never known

Success so huge and wholly farcical;
  The women shared
The secret like a happy funeral;
While girls, gripping their handbags tighter, stared
At a religious wounding. Free at last,
And loaded with the sum of all they saw,
We hurried towards London, shuffling gouts of steam.
Now fields were building-plots, and poplars cast
Long shadows over major roads, and for
Some fifty minutes, that in time would seem

Just long enough to settle hats and say
  *I nearly died,*
A dozen marriages got under way.
They watched the landscape, sitting side by side
—An Odeon went past, a cooling tower,
And someone running up to bowl—and none
Thought of the others they would never meet
Or how their lives would all contain this hour.
I thought of London spread out in the sun,
Its postal districts packed like squares of wheat:

There we were aimed. And as we raced across
  Bright knots of rail
Past standing Pullmans, walls of blackened moss
Came close, and it was nearly done, this frail
Travelling coincidence; and what it held
Stood ready to be loosed with all the power
That being changed can give. We slowed again,
And as the tightened brakes took hold, there swelled
A sense of falling, like an arrow-shower
Sent out of sight, somewhere becoming rain.

PHILIP LARKIN

# Here

Swerving east, from rich industrial shadows
And traffic all night north; swerving through fields
Too thin and thistled to be called meadows,
And now and then a harsh-named halt, that shields
Workmen at dawn; swerving to solitude
Of skies and scarecrows, haystacks, hares and pheasants,
And the widening river's slow presence,
The piled gold clouds, the shining gull-marked mud,

Gathers to the surprise of a large town:
Here domes and statues, spires and cranes cluster
Beside grain-scattered streets, barge-crowded water,
And residents from raw estates, brought down
The dead straight miles by stealing flat-faced trolleys,
Push through plate-glass swing doors to their desires—
Cheap suits, red kitchen-ware, sharp shoes, iced lollies,
Electric mixers, toasters, washers, driers—

A cut-price crowd, urban yet simple, dwelling
Where only salesmen and relations come
Within a terminate and fishy-smelling
Pastoral of ships up streets, the slave museum,
Tattoo-shops, consulates, grim head-scarfed wives;
And out beyond its mortgaged half-built edges
Fast-shadowed wheat-fields, running high as hedges,
Isolate villages, where removed lives

Loneliness clarifies. Here silence stands
Like heat. Here leaves unnoticed thicken,
Hidden weeds flower, neglected waters quicken,
Luminously-peopled air ascends;
And past the poppies bluish neutral distance
Ends the land suddenly beyond a beach
Of shapes and shingle. Here is unfenced existence:
Facing the sun, untalkative, out of reach.

PHILIP LARKIN

# St Mark's, Cheetham Hill

Designed to dominate the district—
God being nothing if not large
and stern, melancholic from man's fall
(like Victoria widowed early)—
the church, its yard, were raised on a plateau
six feet above the surrounding green.
There weren't many houses then; Manchester
was a good walk away. I've seen
faded photographs: the church standing
amidst strolling gentry, as though
ready to sail for the Empire's farthest parts;—
the union jack at the tower's masthead
enough to quell upstart foreigners and natives.
But those were the early days. The city
began to gollop profits, burst
outward on all sides. Soon,
miles of the cheapest brick swaddled landmarks,
the church one. Chimes that had used to wake
workers in Whitefield, died in near streets.

From our house—a part of the parish—
St. Mark's is a turn right, a turn left,
and straight down Coke Street past the Horseshoe.
The raised graveyard—full these many years—
overlooks the junction of five streets;
pollarded plane trees round its edge,
the railings gone to help fight Hitler.
Adam Murray of New Galloway,
'Who much improved the spinning mule',
needs but a step from his tomb to peer in
at somebody's glittering television;
Harriet Pratt, 'A native of Derby',
might sate her judgement-hunger with chips
were she to rise and walk twenty yards.
The houses are that close. The church,
begrimed, an ugly irregular box
squatting above those who once filled it
with faith and praise, looks smaller now
than in those old pictures. Subdued
by a raincoat factory's bulk, the Kosher

Slaughter House next door, its dignity
is rare weddings, the Co-op hearse,
and hired cars full of elderly mourners.
The congregations are tiny these days;
few folk could tell you whether it's 'High' or 'Low';
the vicar's name, the times of services,
is specialized knowledge. And fear has gone;
the damp, psalmed, God of my childhood has gone.
Perhaps a boy delivering papers
in winter darkness before the birds wake,
keeps to Chapel Street's far side, for fear
some corpse interred at his ankle's depth
might shove a hand through the crumbling wall
and grab him in passing; but not for fear
of black religion—the blurred bulk
of God in drizzle and dirty mist,
or hooded with snow on his white throne
watching the sparrow fall.
                              Now, the graveyard,
its elegant wrought-ironwork wrenched,
carted away; its rhymed epitaphs,
urns of stone and ingenious scrolls,
chipped, tumbled, masked by weeds,
is used as a playground. Shouting children
Tiggy between the tombs.
                              On Saturdays
I walk there sometimes—through the drift
of jazz from open doors, the tide
of frying fish, and the groups of women
gossiping on their brushes—to see the church,
its God decamped, or dead, or daft
to all but the shrill hosannas of children
whose prayers are laughter, playing such parts
in rowdy games, you'd think it built
for no greater purpose, think its past
one long term of imprisonment.

There's little survives Authority's cant
that's not forgotten, written-off,
or misunderstood. The Methodist Chapel's
been bought by the Jews for a Synagogue;
Ukrainian Catholics have the Wesleyan's
sturdy structure built to outlast Rome—
and men of the district say St. Mark's
is part of a clearance area. Soon
it will be down as low as rubble
from every house that squeezed it round,
to bed a motorway and a new estate.
Or worse: repainted, pointed, primmed—
as becomes a unit in town-planners'
clever dreams of a healthy community—
will prosper in dignity and difference,
the gardened centre of new horizons.

Rather than this, I'd see it smashed,
and picture the final splendours of decay:
Opposing gangs in wild 'Relievo',
rushing down aisles and dusty pews
at which the houses look straight in
past broken wall; and late-night drunkards
stumbling their usual short-cut home
across uneven eulogies, fumbling
difficult flies to pour discomfort out
in comfortable shadows, in a nave
they praise with founts, and moonlit blooms of steam.

TONY CONNOR

# Birches

When I see birches bend to left and right
Across the lines of straighter darker trees,
I like to think some boy's been swinging on them.
But swinging doesn't bend them down to stay
As ice-storms do. Often you must have seen them
Loaded with ice a sunny winter morning
After a rain. They click upon themselves
As the breeze rises, and turn many-coloured
As the stir cracks and crazes their enamel.
Soon the sun's warmth makes them shed their crystal shells
Shattering and avalanching on the snow-crust—
Such heaps of broken glass to sweep away
You'd think the inner dome of heaven had fallen.
They are dragged to the withered bracken by the load,
And they seem not to break; though once they are bowed
So low for long, they never right themselves:
You may see their trunks arching in the woods
Years afterwards, trailing their leaves on the ground
Like girls on hands and knees that throw their hair
Before them over their heads to dry in the sun.
But I was going to say when Truth broke in
With all her matter-of-fact about the ice-storm
I should prefer to have some boy bend them
As he went out and in to fetch the cows—
Some boy too far from town to learn basketball,
Whose only play was what he found himself,
Summer or winter, and could play alone.
One by one he subdued his father's trees
By riding them down over and over again
Until he took the stiffness out of them,
And not one but hung limp, not one was left
For him to conquer. He learned all there was
To learn about not launching out too soon
And so not carrying the tree away
Clear to the ground. He always kept his poise
To the top branches, climbing carefully
With the same pains you use to fill a cup
Up to the brim, and even above the brim.
Then he flung outward, feet first, with a swish,
Kicking his way down through the air to the ground.

So was I once myself a swinger of birches.
And so I dream of going back to be.
It's when I'm weary of considerations,
And life is too much like a pathless wood
Where your face burns and tickles with the cobwebs
Broken across it, and one eye is weeping
From a twig's having lashed across it open.
I'd like to get away from earth awhile
And then come back to it and begin over.
May no fate wilfully misunderstand me
And half grant what I wish and snatch me away
Not to return. Earth's the right place for love:
I don't know where it's likely to go better.
I'd like to go by climbing a birch tree,
And climb black branches up a snow-white trunk
Toward heaven till the tree could bear no more,
But dipped its top and set me down again.
That would be good both going and coming back.
One could do worse than be a swinger of birches.

ROBERT FROST

# Thistles

Against the rubber tongues of cows and the hoeing hands of
  men
Thistles spike the summer air
Or crackle open under a blue-black pressure.

Every one a revengeful burst
Of resurrection, a grasped fistful
Of splintered weapons and Icelandic frost thrust up

From the underground stain of a decayed Viking.
They are like pale hair and the gutturals of dialects.
Every one manages a plume of blood.

Then they grow grey, like men.
Mown down, it is a feud. Their sons appear,
Stiff with weapons, fighting back over the same ground.

TED HUGHES

# After Apple-Picking

My long two-pointed ladder's sticking through a tree
Toward heaven still,
And there's a barrel that I didn't fill
Beside it, and there may be two or three
Apples I didn't pick upon some bough.
But I am done with apple-picking now.
Essence of winter sleep is on the night,
The scent of apples: I am drowsing off.
I cannot rub the strangeness from my sight
I got from looking through a pane of glass
I skimmed this morning from the drinking trough
And held against the world of hoary grass.
It melted, and I let it fall and break.

But I was well
Upon my way to sleep before it fell,
And I could tell
What form my dreaming was about to take
Magnified apples appear and disappear,
Stem end and blossom end,
And every fleck of russet showing clear.
My instep arch not only keeps the ache,
It keeps the pressure of a ladder-round.
I feel the ladder sway as the boughs bend.
And I keep hearing from the cellar bin
The rumbling sound
Of load on load of apples coming in.
For I have had too much
Of apple-picking: I am overtired
Of the great harvest I myself desired.
There were ten thousand thousand fruit to touch,
Cherish in hand, lift down, and not let fall.
For all
That struck the earth,
No matter if not bruised or spiked with stubble,
Went sure to the cider-apple heap
As of no worth.
One can see what will trouble
This sleep of mine, whatever sleep it is.
Were he not gone,
The woodchuck could say whether it's like his
Long sleep, as I describe its coming on,
Or just some human sleep.

ROBERT FROST

# Mountain Limestone

Out of their shells the sea-beasts creep
     And eels un-reel from holes;
With eyes of stone they stare and weep
     Green stalactites of tears;
     On sea-washed caves of years
The temporal tide reclines and rolls,
And miser mussels, packed and pearled,
Lie like a clutch of peewit's eggs
     In the stone conger's coils,
     Looped around the world.

Where flimsy clints are scraped bone-bare
     A whale's ribs glint in the sun,
Coral has built bright islands there,
And birch and juniper fin the fell,
Dark as a trawling under-wave,
With rockrose opening three
Green hands that cup the flower,
And chiselled clean on stone
A spider-web of shell,
The thumb-print of the sea.                    NORMAN NICHOLSON


# Pennines in April

If this country were a sea (that is solid rock
Deeper than any sea) these hills heaving
Out of the east, mass behind mass, at this height
Hoisting heather and stones to the sky
Must burst upwards and topple into Lancashire.

Perhaps, as the earth turns, such ground-stresses
Do come rolling westward through the locked land.
Now, measuring the miles of silence
Your eye takes the strain: through

Landscapes gliding blue as water
Those barrellings of strength are heaving slowly and heave
To your feet and surf upwards
In a still, fiery air, hauling the imagination,
Carrying the larks upward.                    TED HUGHES

* **Performances.** Groups or individuals rehearse the following poems for performance, live or taped.

—*Not Waving But Drowning* (page 34) can be shared between two voices, a narrator and a second voice to speak lines 3 and 4, 9, 11 and 12.

—*Daft Annie On Our Village Mainstreet* (page 30) can be read by three voices, each taking a section and combining in the last two lines for her epitaph.

—In *City Johannesburg* (page 38) the writer gives a migrant worker's view of the city. The phrase 'Jo'burg City' runs through the poem as a refrain. A performance could have a group speaking this phrase and a single voice for the rest. Think carefully about the tone of the poem and the feelings it expresses.

—*Skanking Englishman Between Trains* (page 35) can be spoken by two voices. It has a repeated chorus in sections 2, 4 and 6. Go for the reggae rhythm in these lines.

* **Landmarks.** Tony Connor's poem on page 43 describes a building which has a special significance for him—St. Mark's Church. Perhaps there is a particular local landmark or area which you know well—a park, a church, a ruin, a monument, a radio mast—there are many possibilities here. Once you have chosen your subject try to capture its shape, colour and character in detail: if it has any special associations for you—maybe from years ago—include these in your poem.

* **Pictures with Poems.** Step into the picture *Approach to a Village* (pages 50–51). The long shadows suggest it's late afternoon in summer or autumn. Jot down words, phrases and comparisons to capture the atmosphere you find there and develop them into a short poem.

—Look at the details of the photograph of harvesting in Kent (page 53). You could begin a poem 'Seen from above . . .' and list the details and comparisons that the picture suggests to you.

* **Self-portraits.** *Poem in October* (page 26) and *Phenomenal Woman* (page 36) are both celebratory poems, written in the first person. Hear them read aloud and talk about the feelings they express. You could try your own birthday poem, or write 'Phenomenal Man'.

# Is Love The Answer?

## Riddle-Me-Ree

My first is in life (not contained within heart)
My second's in whole but never in part.
My third's in forever, but also in vain.
My last's in ending, why not in pain?

is love the answer?

LIZ LOCHHEAD

## Sonnet 116

Let me not to the marriage of true minds
Admit impediments. Love is not love
Which alters when it alteration finds,
Or bends with the remover to remove.
O, no! it is an ever-fixed mark,
That looks on tempests and is never shaken;
It is the star to every wand'ring bark,
Whose worth's unknown, although his height be taken.
Love's not Time's fool, though rosy lips and cheeks
Within his bending sickle's compass come;
Love alters not with his brief hours and weeks,
But bears it out even to the edge of doom.
   If this be error, and upon me prov'd,
   I never writ, nor no man ever lov'd.

WILLIAM SHAKESPEARE

# He Wishes for the Cloths of Heaven

Had I the heavens' embroidered cloths,
Enwrought with golden and silver light,
The blue and the dim and the dark cloths
Of night and light and the half-light,
I would spread the cloths under your feet:
But I, being poor, have only my dreams;
I have spread my dreams under your feet;
Tread softly because you tread on my dreams.

W. B. YEATS

# Plucking the Rushes

Garden rushes with red shoots,
Long leaves bending to the wind—
You and I in the same boat
Plucking rushes at the Five Lakes.
We started at dawn from the orchid-island;
We rested under the elms till noon.
You and I plucking rushes
Had not plucked a handful when night came!

ANON. (trans. Arthur Waley)

56

# The Picnic

It is the picnic with Ruth in the spring.
Ruth was the third on my list of seven girls
But the first two were gone (Betty) or else
Had someone (Ellen had accepted Doug).
Indian Gully the last day of school;
Girls make the lunches for the boys too.
I wrote a note to Ruth in algebra class
Day before the test. She smiled, and nodded.
We left the cars and walked through the young corn
The shoots green as paint and the leaves like tongues
Trembling. Beyond the fence where we stood
Some wild strawberry flowered by an elm tree
And Jack-in-the-pulpit was olive ripe.
A blackbird fled as I crossed, and showed
A spot of gold or red under its quick wing.
I held the wire for Ruth and watched the whip
Of her long, striped skirt as she followed.
Three freckles blossomed on her thin, white back
Underneath the loop where the blouse buttoned.
We went for our lunch away from the rest,
Stretched in the new grass, our heads close
Over unknown things wrapped up in wax papers.
Ruth tried for the same, I forget what it was,
And our hands were together. She laughed,
And a breeze caught the edge of her brown, loose hair
That touched my cheek. I turned my face into
The gentle fall. I saw how sweet it smelled.
She didn't move her head or take her hand.
I felt a soft caving in my stomach
As at the top of the highest slide
When I had been a child, but was not afraid,
And did not know why my eyes moved with wet
As I brushed her cheek with my lips and brushed
Her lips with my own lips. She said to me
Jack, Jack, different than I had ever heard,
Because she wasn't calling me, I think,
Or telling me. She used my name to
Talk in another way I wanted to know.
She laughed again and then she took her hand;
I gave her what we both had touched—can't

Remember what it was, and we ate the lunch.
Afterwards we walked in the small, cool creek
Our shoes off, her skirt hitched, and she smiling,
My pants rolled, and then we climbed up the high
Side of Indian Gully and looked
Where we had been, our hands together again.
It was then some bright thing came in my eyes,
Starting at the back of them and flowing
Suddenly through my head and down my arms
And stomach and my bare legs that seemed not
To stop in feet, nor to feel the red earth
Of the Gully, as though we hung in a
Touch of birds. There was a word in my throat
With the feeling and I knew the first time
What it meant and I said, it's beautiful.
Yes, she said, and I felt the sound and word
In my hand join the sound and word in hers
As in one name said, or in one cupped hand.
We put back on our shoes and socks and we
Sat in the grass awhile, crosslegged, under
A blowing tree, not saying anything.
And Ruth played with shells she found in the creek,
As I watched. Her small wrist which was so sweet
To me turned by her breast and the shells dropped
Green, white, blue, easily into her lap,
Passing light through themselves. She gave the pale
Shells to me, and got up and touched her hips
With her light hands, and we walked down slowly
To play the school games with the others.

JOHN LOGAN

# Anancy's Thoughts on Love

*(Anancy is a trickster spider man figure traditional to Caribbean folk tales)*

Love got teeth
as old people say
dont know if you walking
on you hand or you feet
but it dont really matter
cause you bound to meet
sooner or later

love is watching hint
big and bold
but refusing to catch it

love is trapping thoughts
in side-eye gaze
long before thoughts see light-of-day

love is sweet mystery
like sleight-of-rain

But love is sweet misery
like taste of pain

love is going down winding labyrinth
at loss for words
and loss of head
but Anancy thank God
always have piece of thread
for way back out

or to put it another way
Anancy in love
always save back piece of heart
for peace of mind

JOHN AGARD

# Rapunzstiltskin

& just when our maiden had got
good & used to her isolation,
stopped daily expecting to be rescued,
had come to almost love her tower,
along comes This Prince
with absolutely
all the wrong answers.
Of course she had not been brought up to look for
originality or gingerbread
so at first she was quite undaunted
by his tendency to talk in strung-together cliché.
'Just hang on and we'll get you out of there'
he hollered like a fireman in some soap opera
when she confided her plight (the old
hag inside etc. & how trapped she was);
well, it was corny but
he did look sort of gorgeous
axe and all.
So there she was, humming & pulling
all the pins out of her chignon,
throwing him all the usual lifelines
till, soon, he was shimmying in & out
every other day as though
he owned the place, bringing her
the sex manuals & skeins of silk
from which she was meant, eventually,
to weave the means of her own escape.
'All very well & good,' she prompted,
'but when exactly?'
She gave him till
well past the bell on the timeclock.
She mouthed at him, hinted,
she was keener than a T.V. quizmaster
that he should get it right.
'I'll do everything in my power' he intoned, 'but
the impossible (she groaned) might
take a little longer.' He grinned.
She pulled her glasses off.
'All the better
to see you with my dear?' he hazarded.

She screamed, cut off her hair.
'Why, you're beautiful?' he guessed tentatively.
'No, No, No!' she
shrieked & stamped her foot so
hard it sank six cubits through the floorboards.
'I love you?' he came up with
as finally she tore herself in two.

LIZ LOCHHEAD

# First Love

I ne'er was struck before that hour
   With love so sudden and so sweet.
   Her face it bloomed like a sweet flower
   And stole my heart away complete.
My face turned pale as deadly pale,
   My legs refused to walk away,
And when she looked 'what could I ail?'
   My life and all seemed turned to clay.

And then my blood rushed to my face
   And took my sight away.
The trees and bushes round the place
   Seemed midnight at noonday.
I could not see a single thing,
   Words from my eyes did start;
They spoke as chords do from the string,
   And blood burnt round my heart.

Are flowers the winter's choice?
   Is love's bed always snow?
She seemed to hear my silent voice
   And love's appeal to know.

I never saw so sweet a face
   As that I stood before:
My heart has left its dwelling-place
   And can return no more.

JOHN CLARE

# Mole Love

The lover

The mole of love tunnels beneath the rose;
Peculiar roots tickle his ram-rod nose.

The flirt

An expert in the arts of purblind love
Winks through the fingers of his velvet glove.

Mole lust

These pock-marks, blotched like craters on the moon,
Erupt in soiled lust from earth's cocoon.

The sensualist

A mole upon the shoulder of this hill
Excites the valleys to a springtime thrill.

The aesthete

His earthly orbit done, exhausted mole
Lies back to watch the heavenly bodies roll.

The wit

I thought all creatures were without a soul
Until I met this curious animole.

Mole's temptation

The hole of love lies open in the grass
Inviting mole to be made whole or pass.

The philosopher

He shovels back the future with his paws
Convinced of the effect if not the cause.

ROSE BENNETT

# Night Ride

Along the black
leather strap
of the night
deserted road

swiftly rolls
the freighted bus.
Huddled together
two lovers doze

their hands linkt
across their laps
their bodies loosely
interlockt

their heads resting
two heavy fruits
on the plaited
basket of their limbs.

Slowly the bus
slides into light.
Here are hills
detach'd from dark

the road, uncoils
a white ribbon
the lovers with
the hills unfold

wake cold
to face the fate
of those who love
despite the world.

HERBERT READ

# Dog-Tired

If she would come to me here
    Now the sunken swaths
    Are glittering paths
To the sun, and the swallows cut clear
Into the setting sun! if she came to me here!

If she would come to me now,
Before the last-mown harebells are dead
While that vetch clump still burns red!
Before all the bats have dropped from the bough
To cool in the night; if she came to me now!

The horses are untackled, the chattering machine
Is still at last. If she would come
We could gather up the dry hay from
The hill-brow, and lie quite still, till the green
Sky ceased to quiver, and lost its active sheen.

I should like to drop
On the hay, with my head on her knee,
And lie dead still, while she
Breathed quiet above me; and the crop
Of stars grew silently.

I should like to lie still
As if I was dead; but feeling
Her hand go stealing
Over my face and my head, until
This ache was shed.

D. H. LAWRENCE

# Les Sylphides

Life in a day: he took his girl to the ballet;
Being shortsighted himself could hardly see it—
    The white skirts in the grey
    Glade and the swell of the music
    Lifting the white sails.

Calyx upon calyx, canterbury bells in the breeze
The flowers on the left mirror to the flowers on the right
    And the naked arms above
    The powdered faces moving
    Like seaweed in a pool.

Now, he thought, we are floating—ageless, oarless—
Now there is no separation, from now on
    You will be wearing white
    Satin and a red sash
    Under the waltzing trees.

But the music stopped, the dancers took their curtain,
The river had come to a lock—a shuffle of programmes—
    And we cannot continue down
    Stream unless we are ready
    To enter the lock and drop.

So they were married—to be the more together—
And found they were never again so much together,
    Divided by the morning tea,
    By the evening paper,
    By children and the tradesmen's bills.

Waking at times in the night she found assurance
In his regular breathing, but wondered whether
    It was really worth it and where
    The river had flowed away
    And where were the white flowers.

LOUIS MACNEICE

# One Flesh

Lying apart now, each in a separate bed,
  He with a book, keeping the light on late,
She like a girl dreaming of childhood,
  All men elsewhere—it is as if they wait
Some new event: the book he holds unread,
Her eyes fixed on the shadows overhead.

Tossed up like flotsam from a former passion,
  How cool they lie. They hardly ever touch,
Or if they do it is like a confession
  Of having little feeling—or too much.
Chastity faces them, a destination
For which their whole lives were a preparation.

Strangely apart and strangely close together,
  Silence between them like a thread to hold
And not wind in. And time itself's a feather
  Touching them gently. Do they know they're old,
These two who are my father and mother
Whose fire, from which I came, has now grown cold?

ELIZABETH JENNINGS

# Made in Heaven

From Heals and Harrods come her lovely bridegrooms
(One cheque alone furnished two bedrooms),

From a pantechnicon in the dog-paraded street
Under the orange plane leaves, on workmen's feet

Crunching over Autumn, the fruits of marriage brought
Craftsmen-felt wood, Swedish dressers, a court

Stool tastefully imitated and the wide bed—
(the girl who married money kept her maiden head).

As things were ticked off the Harrods list, there grew
A middle-class maze to pick your way through—

The labour-saving kitchen to match the labour-saving thing
She'd fitted before marriage (O Love, with this ring

I thee wed)—lastly the stereophonic radiogram
And her Aunt's sly letter promising a pram.

Settled in now, the Italian honeymoon over,
As the relatives said, she was living in clover.

The discontented drinking of a few weeks stopped,
She woke up one morning to her husband's alarm-clock,

Saw the shining faces of the wedding gifts from the bed,
Foresaw the cosy routine of the massive years ahead.

As she watched her husband knot his tie for the city,
She thought: I wanted to be a dancer once—it's a pity

I've done none of the things I thought I wanted to,
Found nothing more exacting than my own looks, got through

Half a dozen lovers whose faces I can't quite remember
(I can still start the Rose Adagio, one foot on the fender)

But at least I'm safe from everything but cancer—
The apotheosis of the young wife and mediocre dancer.

PETER PORTER

# The Passionate Shepherd to his Love

Come live with me and be my Love,
And we will all the pleasures prove
That hills and valleys, dale and field,
And all the craggy mountains yield.

There will we sit upon the rocks
And see the shepherds feed their flocks,
By shallow rivers, to whose falls
Melodious birds sing madrigals.

There will I make thee beds of roses
And a thousand fragrant posies,
A cap of flowers and a kirtle
Embroidered all with leaves of myrtle.

A gown made of the finest wool,
Which from our pretty lambs we pull,
Fair linèd slippers for the cold,
With buckles of the purest gold.

A belt of straw and ivy buds
With coral clasps and amber studs:
And if these pleasures may thee move,
Come live with me and be my Love.

Thy silver dishes for thy meat
As precious as the gods do eat,
Shall on an ivory table be
Prepared each day for thee and me.

The shepherd swains shall dance and sing
For thy delight each May-morning:
If these delights thy mind may move,
Then live with me and be my Love.

CHRISTOPHER MARLOWE

# The Sunne Rising

Busie old foole, unruly Sunne,
Why dost thou thus,
Through windowes, and through curtaines call on us?
Must to thy motions lovers seasons run?
Sawcy pedantique wretch, goe chide
Late schoole boyes and sowre prentices,
Go tell Court-huntsmen, that the King will ride,
Call countrey ants to harvest offices;
Love, all alike, no season knowes, nor clyme,
Nor houres, dayes, moneths, which are the rags of time.

Thy beames, so reverend, and strong
Why shouldst thou thinke?
I could eclipse and cloud them with a winke,
But that I would not lose her sight so long:
If her eyes have not blinded thine,
Looke, and tomorrow late, tell mee,
Whether both th'India's of spice and Myne
Be where thou leftest them, or lie here with mee.
Aske for those Kings whom thou saw'st yesterday,
And thou shalt heare, All here in one bed lay.

She is all States, and all Princes, I,
Nothing else is.
Princes doe but play us; compar'd to this,
All honour's mimique; All wealth alchimie.
Thou sunne art halfe as happy as wee,
In that the world's contracted thus;
Thine age askes ease, and since thy duties bee
To warme the world, that's done in warming us.
Shine here to us, and thou art every where;
This bed thy center is, these walls, thy spheare.

JOHN DONNE

# To His Coy Mistress

Had we but World enough, and Time,
This coyness Lady were no crime.
We would sit down, and think which way
To walk, and pass our long Loves Day.
Thou by the *Indian Ganges* side
Should'st Rubies find: I by the Tide
Of *Humber* would complain. I would
Love you ten years before the Flood:
And you should if you please refuse
Till the Conversion of the *Jews*.
My vegetable Love should grow
Vaster than Empires, and more slow.
An hundred years should go to praise
Thine Eyes, and on thy Forehead Gaze.
Two hundred to adore each Breast:
But thirty thousand to the rest.
An Age at least to every part,
And the last Age should show your Heart.
For Lady you deserve this State;
Nor would I love at lower rate.
   But at my back I alwaies hear
Times winged Charriot hurrying near:
And yonder all before us lye
Desarts of vast Eternity.
Thy Beauty shall no more be found,
Nor, in thy marble Vault, shall sound
My ecchoing Song: then Worms shall try
That long preserv'd Virginity:
And your quaint Honour turn to dust;
And into ashes all my Lust.
The Grave's a fine and private Place,
But none I think do there embrace.
   Now therefore, while the youthful hew
Sits on thy skin like morning dew,
And while thy willing Soul transpires
At every pore with instant Fires,
Now let us sport us while we may;
And now, like am'rous birds of prey,
Rather at once our Time devour,
Than languish in his slow-chapt pow'r.

Let us roll all our Strength, and all
Our sweetness, up into one Ball:
And tear our Pleasures with rough strife,
Thorough the Iron gates of Life.
Thus, though we cannot make our Sun
Stand still, yet we will make him run.

ANDREW MARVELL

## When You Are Old

When you are old and grey and full of sleep,
And nodding by the fire, take down this book,
And slowly read, and dream of the soft look
Your eyes had once, and of their shadows deep.

How many loved your moments of glad grace,
And loved your beauty with love false or true,
But one man loved the pilgrim soul in you,
And loved the sorrows of your changing face;

And bending down beside the glowing bars,
Murmur, a little sadly, how Love fled
And paced upon the mountains overhead
And hid his face amid a crowd of stars.

W. B. YEATS

# Neutral Tones

We stood by a pond that winter day,
And the sun was white, as though chidden of God,
And a few leaves lay on the starving sod,
    —They had fallen from an ash, and were gray.

Your eyes on me were as eyes that rove
Over tedious riddles solved years ago;
And words played between us to and fro—
    On which lost the more by our love.

The smile on your mouth was the deadest thing
Alive enough to have strength to die;
And a grin of bitterness swept thereby
    Like an ominous bird a-wing . . .

Since then, keen lessons that love deceives,
And wrings with wrong, have shaped to me
Your face, and the God-curst sun, and a tree,
    And a pond edged with grayish leaves.

                                        THOMAS HARDY


# The Parting

Since there's no help, come let us kiss and part—
Nay, I have done, you get no more of me;
And I am glad, yea, glad with all my heart,
That thus so cleanly I myself can free.
Shake hands for ever, cancel all our vows,
And when we meet at any time again,
Be it not seen in either of our brows
That we one jot of former love retain.
Now at the last gasp of Love's latest breath,
When, his pulse failing, Passion speechless lies,
When Faith is kneeling by his bed of death,
And Innocence is closing up his eyes,
    —Now if thou wouldst, when all have given him over,
    From death to life thou might'st him yet recover.

                                        MICHAEL DRAYTON

# Intimates

Don't you care for my love? she said bitterly.

I handed her the mirror, and said:
Please address these questions to the proper person!
Please make all requests to head-quarters!
In all matters of emotional importance
please approach the supreme authority direct!—
So I handed her the mirror.

And she would have broken it over my head,
but she caught sight of her own reflection
and that held her spellbound for two seconds
while I fled.

D. H. LAWRENCE

★ **Attraction.** John Logan's poem *The Picnic* (p. 57) describes an occasion when, for the first time, Jack, a teenager, feels some real sympathy and affection flow between himself and a girl whom he has taken on the school picnic. Notice how the writer makes the incident believable by describing carefully *in detail* the land-scape of Indian Gully, the ordinary activities of picnicking, walk-ing in the river or playing with shells, and the special feeling of attraction and happiness which develops between two people. (Munch's picture, *Attraction* (p. 58) catches the same sort of feeling).

There may be a similar experience, real or imagined, which you could write about. It's often best to approach such feelings indirectly, so one way to start is simply by making a list of details of your experience or anecdote and letting your feelings and thoughts gather round these items.

* **Ideal Images.** How much does your image of an ideal boy or girl friend owe to the media, or to the romances of magazines? *In pairs*, list all the characteristics that typically go to make up these ideal images. Then make two more corresponding lists of all the *opposite* qualities. From these second lists you should be able to develop two satirical portraits—anti-romantic images which 'send up' the conventional ideas of the ideal boy or girl friend.

* **Observation.** Herbert Read's *Night Ride* (p. 64) may remind you of an occasion when you have noticed two people showing their affection for each other quite naturally and unself-consciously. Perhaps the turn of a head, a particular look in someone's eyes, a kiss, the holding of hands may have struck you as beautiful. Make a brief word-picture that sums up for you the love that lies between people. You could write it as a haiku for example, or in couplet form as in *Mole Love* (p. 63).

* **Songs.** There are a great many songs about love relationships. In a lot of them the music is far more important than the lyrics, but you may know some where the words are effective on their own. A group of you could make your own anthology of lyrics on a theme of your choice.

* **Dialogues.** One situation you may have faced already and which you are almost certain to face in the future is visiting the boy or girl friend's home for the first time and meeting his or her parents. There is scope for a piece of writing here based on such a situation, either real or imagined. In pairs, invent a short scene, setting out the dialogue in the form of a play. Some of these playlets could be acted out or tape-recorded.

War

# Futility

Move him into the sun—
Gently its touch awoke him once,
At home, whispering of fields unsown.
Always it woke him, even in France,
Until this morning and this snow.
If anything might rouse him now
The kind old sun will know.

Think how it wakes the seeds,—
Woke, once, the clays of a cold star.
Are limbs, so dear-achieved, are sides,
Full-nerved—still warm—too hard to stir?
Was it for this the clay grew tall?
—O what made fatuous sunbeams toil
To break earth's sleep at all?

WILFRED OWEN

# Disabled

He sat in a wheeled chair, waiting for dark,
And shivered in his ghastly suit of grey,
Legless, sewn short at elbow. Through the park
Voices of boys rang saddening like a hymn,
Voices of play and pleasure after day,
Till gathering sleep had mothered them from him.

About this time Town used to swing so gay
When glow-lamps budded in the light blue trees,
And girls glanced lovelier as the air grew dim,—
In the old times, before he threw away his knees.
Now he will never feel again how slim
Girls' waists are, or how warm their subtle hands;
All of them touch him like some queer disease.

There was an artist silly for his face,
For it was younger than his youth, last year.
Now, he is old; his back will never brace;
He's lost his colour very far from here,
Poured it down shell-holes till the veins ran dry,
And half his lifetime lapsed in the hot race,
And leap of purple spurted from his thigh.

One time he liked a blood-smear down his leg,
After the matches, carried shoulder-high.
It was after football, when he'd drunk a peg,
He thought he'd better join.—He wonders why.
Someone had said he'd look a god in kilts,
That's why; and may be, too, to please his Meg;
Aye, that was it, to please the giddy jilts
He asked to join. He didn't have to beg;
Smiling they wrote his lie; aged nineteen years.
Germans he scarcely thought of; all their guilt,
And Austria's, did not move him. And no fears
Of Fear came yet. He thought of jewelled hilts
For daggers in plaid socks; of smart salutes;
And care of arms; and leave; and pay arrears;
*Esprit de corps*; and hints for young recruits.
And soon, he was drafted out with drums and cheers.

Some cheered him home, but not as crowds cheer Goal.
Only a solemn man who brought him fruits
*Thanked* him; and then inquired about his soul.

Now, he will spend a few sick years in Institutes,
And do what things the rules consider wise,
And take whatever pity they may dole.
To-night he noticed how the women's eyes
Passed from him to the strong men that were whole.
How cold and late it is! Why don't they come
And put him into bed? Why don't they come?

WILFRED OWEN

Daddy, what did _YOU_ do in the Great War?

## 'Blighters'

The House is crammed: tier beyond tier they grin
And cackle at the Show, while prancing ranks
Of harlots shrill the chorus, drunk with din;
'We're sure the Kaiser loves our dear old Tanks!'

I'd like to see a Tank come down the stalls,
Lurching to rag-time tunes, or 'Home, sweet Home',
And there'd be no more jokes in Music-halls
To mock the riddled corpses round Bapaume.

SIEGFRIED SASSOON

## The General

'Good-morning; good-morning!' the General said
When we met him last week on our way to the line.
Now the soldiers he smiled at are most of 'em dead,
And we're cursing his staff for incompetent swine.
'He's a cheery old card,' grunted Harry to Jack
As they slogged up to Arras with rifle and pack.

. . . . . . . . . .

But he did for them both by his plan of attack.

SIEGFRIED SASSOON

# Lamentations

I found him in the guard-room at the Base.
From the blind darkness I had heard his crying
And blundered in. With puzzled, patient face
A sergeant watched him; it was no good trying
To stop it; for he howled and beat his chest.
And, all because his brother had gone west,
Raved at the bleeding war; his rampant grief
Moaned, shouted, sobbed, and choked, while he was kneeling
Half-naked on the floor. In my belief
Such men have lost all patriotic feeling.

SIEGFRIED SASSOON

82

# Naming of Parts

Today we have naming of parts. Yesterday,
We had daily cleaning. And tomorrow morning
We shall have what to do after firing. But today,
Today we have naming of parts. Japonica
Glistens like coral in all of the neighbouring gardens,
    And to-day we have naming of parts.

This is the lower sling swivel. And this
Is the upper sling swivel, whose use you will see,
When you are given your slings. And this is the piling swivel,
Which in your case you have not got. The branches
Hold in the gardens their silent, eloquent gestures,
    Which in our case we have not got.

This is the safety-catch, which is always released
With an easy flick of the thumb. And please do not let me
See anyone using his finger. You can do it quite easy
If you have any strength in your thumb. The blossoms
Are fragile and motionless, never letting anyone see
    Any of them using their finger.

And this you can see is the bolt. The purpose of this
Is to open the breech, as you see. We can slide it
Rapidly backwards and forwards: we call this
Easing the spring. And rapidly backwards and forwards
The early bees are assaulting and fumbling the flowers;
    They call it easing the Spring.

They call it easing the Spring: it is perfectly easy
If you have any strength in your thumb: like the bolt,
And the breech, and the cocking-piece, and the point of
  balance,
Which in our case we have not got; and the almond-blossom
Silent in all of the gardens and the bees going backwards and
  forwards,
    For today we have naming of parts.

HENRY REED

# Bayonet Charge

Suddenly he awoke and was running—raw
In raw-seamed hot khaki, his sweat heavy,
Stumbling across a field of clods towards a green hedge
That dazzled with rifle fire, hearing
Bullets smacking the belly out of the air—
He lugged a rifle numb as a smashed arm;
The patriotic tear that had brimmed in his eye
Sweating like molten iron from the centre of his chest,—

In bewilderment then he almost stopped—
In what cold clockwork of the stars and the nations
Was he the hand pointing that second? He was running
Like a man who has jumped up in the dark and runs
Listening between his footfalls for the reason
Of his still running, and his foot hung like
Statuary in mid-stride. Then the shot-slashed furrows

Threw up a yellow hare that rolled like a flame
And crawled in a threshing circle, its mouth wide
Open silent, its eyes standing out.
He plunged past with his bayonet toward the green
    hedge.
King, honour, human dignity, etcetera
Dropped like luxuries in a yelling alarm
To get out of that blue crackling air
His terror's touchy dynamite.

TED HUGHES

# Earlswood

Air-raid shelters at school were damp tunnels
where you sang 'Ten Green Bottles' yet again
and might as well have been doing decimals.

At home, though, it was cosier and more fun:
cocoa and toast inside the Table Shelter,
our iron-panelled bunker, our new den.

By day we ate off it; at night you'd find us
under it, the floor plump with mattresses
and the wire grilles neatly latched around us.

You had to be careful not to bump your head;
we padded the hard metal bits with pillows,
then giggled in our glorious social bed.

What could be safer? What could be more romantic
than playing cards by torchlight in a raid?
Odd that it made our mother so neurotic

to hear the sirens; we were quite content—
but slightly cramped once there were four of us,
after we'd taken in old Mrs Brent

from down by the Nag's Head, who'd been bombed out.
She had her arm in plaster, but she managed
to dress herself, and smiled, and seemed all right.

Perhaps I just imagined hearing her
moaning a little in the night, and shaking
splinters of glass out of her long grey hair.

The next week we were sent to Leicestershire.

FLEUR ADCOCK

# Landscape with Figures

I

Perched on a great fall of air
a pilot or angel looking down
on some eccentric chart, a plain
dotted with useless furniture,
discerns dying on the sand vehicles
squashed dead or still entire, stunned
like beetles: scattered wingcases and
legs, heads, appear when the dust settles.
But you who like Thomas come
to poke fingers in the wounds
find monuments and metal posies.
On each disordered tomb
the steel is torn into fronds
by the lunatic explosive.

II

On sand and scrub the dead men wriggle
in their dowdy clothes. They are mimes
who express silence and futile aims
enacting this prone and motionless struggle
at a queer angle to the scenery,
crawling on the boards of the stage like walls,
deaf to the one who opens his mouth and calls
silently. The decor is a horrible tracery
of iron. The eye and mouth of each figure
bear the cosmetic blood and the hectic
colours death has the only list of.
A yard more and my little finger
could trace the maquillage of these stony actors:
I am the figure writhing on the backcloth.

KEITH DOUGLAS

# No More Hiroshimas

At the station exit, my bundle in hand,
Early the winter afternoon's wet snow
Falls thinly round me, out of a crudded sun.
I had forgotten to remember where I was.
Looking about, I see it might be anywhere—
A station, a town like any other in Japan,
Ramshackle, muddy, noisy, drab; a cheerfully
Shallow permanence: peeling concrete, litter, 'Atomic
Lotion, for hair fall-out,' a flimsy department-store;
Racks and towers of neon, flashy over tiled and tilted waves
Of little roofs, shacks cascading lemons and persimmons,
Oranges and dark-red apples, shanties awash with rainbows
Of squid and octopus, shellfish, slabs of tuna, oysters, ice,
Ablaze with fans of soiled nude-picture books
Thumbed abstractedly by schoolboys, with second-hand looks.

The river remains unchanged, sad, refusing rehabilitation.
In this long, wide, empty official boulevard
The new trees are still small, the office blocks
Basely functional, the bridge a slick abstraction.
But the river remains unchanged, sad, refusing rehabilitation.

In the city centre, far from the station's lively squalor,
A kind of life goes on, in cinemas and hi-fi coffee bars,
In the shuffling racket of pin-table palaces and parlours,
The souvenir-shops piled with junk, kimonoed kewpie-dolls,
Models of the bombed Industry Promotion Hall, memorial ruin
Tricked out with glitter-frost and artificial pearls.

Set in an awful emptiness, the modern tourist hotel is trimmed
With jaded Christmas frippery, flatulent balloons; in the hall,
A giant dingy iced caked in the shape of a Cinderella coach.
The contemporary stairs are treacherous, the corridors
Deserted, my room an overheated morgue, the bar in darkness.
Punctually, the electric chimes ring out across the tidy waste
Their doleful public hymn—the tune unrecognizable,
    evangelist.

Here atomic peace is geared to meet the tourist trade.
Let it remain like this, for all the world to see,
Without nobility or loveliness, and dogged with shame
That is beyond all hope of indignation. Anger, too, is dead.
And why should memorials of what was far
From pleasant have the grace that helps us to forget?

In the dying afternoon, I wander dying round the Park of Peace.
It is right, this squat, dead place, with its left-over air
Of an abandoned International Trade and Tourist Fair.
The stunted trees are wrapped in straw against the cold.
The gardeners are old, old women in blue bloomers, white
    aprons,
Survivors weeding the dead brown lawns around the Children's
Monument.

A hideous pile, the Atomic Bomb Explosion Centre, freezing
    cold,
'Includes the Peace Tower, a museum containing
Atomic-melted slates and bricks, photos showing
What the Atomic Desert looked like, and other
Relics of the catastrophe.'

The other relics:
The ones that made me weep;
The bits of burnt clothing,
The stopped watches, the torn shirts.
The twisted buttons,
The stained and tattered vests and drawers,
The ripped kimonos and charred boots,
The white blouse polka-dotted with atomic rain, indelible,
The cotton summer pants the blasted boys crawled home in, to
    bleed
And slowly die.

Remember only these.
They are the memorials we need.

JAMES KIRKUP

# Relative Sadness

Einstein's eyes
were filled with tears
when he heard about Hiroshima.
Mr. Tamihi
had no eyes left
to show his grief.

COLIN ROWBOTHAM

# Your Attention Please

YOUR ATTENTION PLEASE—
The Polar DEW has just warned that
A nuclear rocket strike of
At least one thousand megatons
Has been launched by the enemy
Directly at our major cities.
This announcement will take
Two and a quarter minutes to make,
You therefore have a further
Eight and a quarter minutes
To comply with the shelter
Requirements published in the Civil
Defence Code—section Atomic Attack.
A specially shortened Mass
Will be broadcast at the end
Of this announcement—
Protestant and Jewish services
Will begin simultaneously—
Select your wavelength immediately
According to instructions
In the Defence Code. Do not
Take well-loved pets (including birds)
Into your shelter—they will consume
Fresh air. Leave the old and bed-

Ridden, you can do nothing for them.
Remember to press the sealing
Switch when everyone is in
The shelter. Set the radiation
Aerial, turn on the geiger barometer.
Turn off your Television now.
Turn off your radio immediately
The services end. At the same time
Secure explosion plugs in the ears
Of each member of your family. Take
Down your plasma flasks. Give your children
The pills marked one and two
In the C.D. green container, then put
Them to bed. Do not break
The inside airlock seals until
The radiation All Clear shows
(Watch for the cuckoo in your
Perspex panel), or your District
Touring Doctor rings your bell.
If before this your air becomes
Exhausted or if any of your family
Is critically injured, administer
The capsules marked 'Valley Forge'
(Red pocket in No. 1 Survival Kit)
For painless death. (Catholics
Will have been instructed by their priests
What to do in this eventuality.)
This announcement is ending. Our President
Has already given orders for
Massive retaliation—it will be
Decisive. Some of us may die.
Remember, statistically
It is not likely to be you.
All flags are flying fully dressed
On Government buildings—the sun is
   shining.
Death is the least we have to fear.
We are all in the hands of God,
Whatever happens happens by His will.
Now go quickly to your shelters.

PETER PORTER

91

# The Forest

Among the primary rocks
where the bird spirits
crack the granite seeds
and the tree statues
with their black arms
threaten the clouds,

suddenly
there comes a rumble,
as if history
were being uprooted,

the grass bristles,
boulders tremble,
the earth's surface cracks

and there grows

a mushroom,

immense as life itself,
filled with billions of cells
immense as life itself,
eternal,
watery,

appearing in this world for the first

and last time.

MIROSLAV HOLUB
*(trans. I. Milner and G. Theiner)*

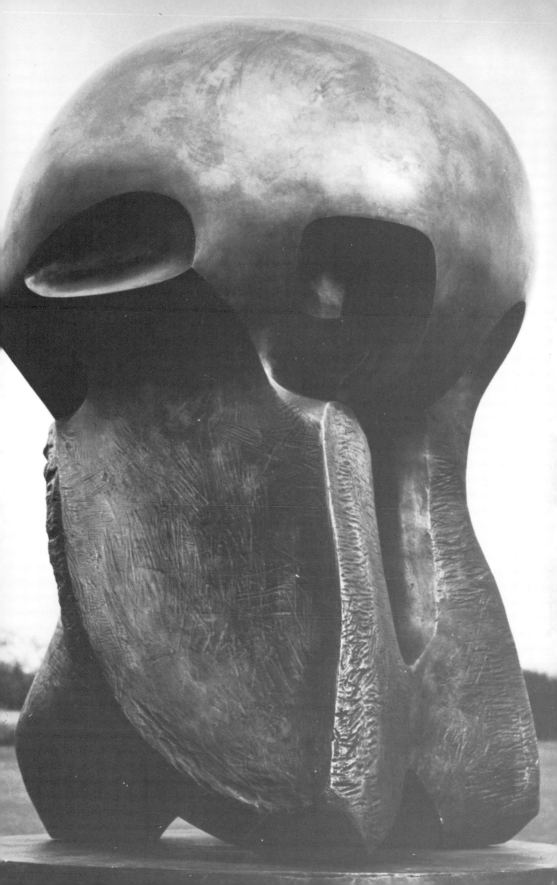

# The Horses

Barely a twelvemonth after
The seven days war that put the world to sleep,
Late in the evening the strange horses came.
By then we had made our covenant with silence,
But in the first few days it was so still
We listened to our breathing and were afraid.
On the second day
The radios failed; we turned the knobs; no answer.
On the third day a warship passed us, heading north,
Dead bodies piled on the deck. On the sixth day
A plane plunged over us into the sea. Thereafter
Nothing. The radios dumb;
And still they stand in corners of our kitchens,
And stand, perhaps, turned on, in a million rooms
All over the world. But now if they should speak,
If on a sudden they should speak again,
If on the stroke of noon a voice should speak,
We would not listen, we would not let it bring
That bad old world that swallowed its children quick
At one great gulp. We would not have it again.
Sometimes we think of the nations lying asleep,
Curled blindly in impenetrable sorrow,
And then the thought confounds us with its strangeness.

The tractors lie about our fields; at evening
They look like dank sea-monsters crouched and waiting.
We leave them where they are and let them rust:
"They'll moulder away and be like other loam."
We make our oxen drag our rusty ploughs,
Long laid aside. We have gone back
Far past our fathers' land.
                              And then, that evening
Late in the summer the strange horses came.
We heard a distant tapping on the road,
A deepening drumming; it stopped, went on again,
And at the corner changed to hollow thunder.

We saw the heads
Like a wild wave charging and were afraid.
We had sold our horses in our fathers' time

94

To buy new tractors. Now they were strange to us
As fabulous steeds set on an ancient shield
Or illustrations in a book of knights.
We did not dare go near them. Yet they waited,
Stubborn and shy, as if they had been sent
By an old command to find our whereabouts
And that long-lost archaic companionship.
In the first moment we had never a thought
That they were creatures to be owned and used.
Among them were some half-a-dozen colts
Dropped in some wilderness of the broken world,
Yet new as if they had come from their own Eden.
Since then they have pulled our ploughs and borne our loads,
But that free servitude still can pierce our hearts.
Our life is changed; their coming our beginning.

EDWIN MUIR

# THE DIFFERENCE BETWEEN ATOMIC AND CONVENTIONAL WEAPONS

Conventional weapons use chemical explosives such as tri-nitrotoluene (TNT) to provide their explosive power, and the power of such weapons is limited simply by the weight of explosive which can be carried. One of the largest conventional weapons to have been developed was the *Grand Slam* used in the Second World War. These bombs each contained about 10 tons of TNT.

In contrast to conventional weapons in which the explosive power is released as a result of chemical reactions, nuclear weapons utilise an entirely different principle. Their power derives from the energy contained within atoms. Such power is enormous, for one pound of plutonium—a material used in the construction of atomic bombs—releases the explosive power equivalent to 8000 tons of TNT.

# EFFECTS OF A ONE-MEGATON NUCLEAR AIRBURST

| | |
|---|---|
| Ground zero | Lethal radiation; most people killed. Almost complete devastation. |
| 2 miles | 50% death. Many survivors will have crush injuries, fractured limbs, internal injuries and/or wounds. Fires ignited cause secondary burns (and possibly firestorms). |
| 4 miles | Flash burns right through skin. Extensive ground damage. |
| 6 miles | Flash burns over approximately 150 square miles; less severe injuries. Structural damage and broken windows. |
| 8 miles | Pressure of 1lb per sq in — wounds from flying glass. |

Scientists have calculated that eight weeks after the start of a 'limited' attack on Britain there would be 72% dead, and 8% injured of the population. (SANA Hard Luck figures 1982)

Source: Joint Committee on the Medical Effects of Nuclear Weapons

# THE GREAT WAR

*THE COST*

In World War I armed forces on both sides totalled 65 million. Of these 8,538,000 were killed and 21,205,000 wounded.

THE ALLIES

5,152,000 dead
12,817,000 wounded

THE ENEMY

3,386,000 dead
8,388,000 wounded

*MANPOWER*

ALLIES:

| | |
|---|---|
| *Russia* | Strength 12 million Killed 1,700,000 |
| *British Empire* | Strength 9 million Killed 908,000 |
| *France* | Strength 8½ million Killed 1,358,000 |
| *Italy* | Strength 5½ million Killed 650,000 |
| *USA* | Strength 4 million Killed 126,000 |

CENTRAL POWERS:

| | |
|---|---|
| *Germany* | Strength 11 million Killed 1,773,000 |
| *Austro-Hungary* | Strength 8 million Killed 1,200,000 |
| *Turkey* | Strength 3 million Killed 325,000 |

*CASUALTIES*

Numerically, Russia, Germany, the Austro-Hungarian Empire and France were the biggest sufferers in men killed, wounded, missing or taken prisoner. But the loss to the British Empire was comparatively just as heavy:
12 per cent of the adult male population of Britain
10 per cent of the adult male population of New Zealand
9 per cent of the adult male population of Australia
6 per cent of the adult male population of Canada were casualties.

*LIFE EXPECTATION*

Life expectation for officers at the front was about 5 months in 1914; about 10 months in 1918
For every officer killed
20 men were killed
Average British casualties a month:

| | Officers | All Ranks |
|---|---|---|
| 1914 | 900 | 18,450 |
| 1915 | 925 | 19,000 |
| 1916 | 2154 | 44,000 |
| 1917 | 2766 | 56,800 |
| 1918 | 3680 | 75,500 |

At the Battle of the Somme on July 1, 1916, the British lost 15 men killed and 25 men wounded a minute for 24 hours

*PRISONERS*

The ALLIES took 3,600,000—2¼ million Austro-Hungarians and over 1 million Germans

The ENEMY took 4 million—2½ million from Russia
½ million from Italy
½ million from France
and fewer than 200,000 from the British Empire

Siegfried Sassoon and Wilfred Owen were probably the two best-known poets of the First World War. Sassoon survived the conflict: Owen was to die by a sniper's bullet in the last stages of the war aged only twenty-five. The two writers had met in hospital where Sassoon, the elder, helped and advised the younger man with his writing. Both were concerned to set down their feelings about the appalling waste of young lives and to capture what they could of the pity, terror and horror of their experiences for those who remained in the relative safety of home.

★ **Performing.** In pairs, read Sassoon's three short poems *Blighters, The General* and *Lamentations* on pages 80–82. They are all pieces that can be dramatised and the first two particularly lend themselves to being shared by different voices. All three poems are bitter and ironic comments on aspects of Sassoon's personal experience; the tatty music-hall act back home which shows no comprehension of the scale of the tragedy being played out in Europe; the incompetent leadership which sent so many young men to their deaths; the total lack of compassion shown by some in the face of individual loss.

Try to put these three poems and one or two of the Owen pieces into a short tape recording or live performance that conveys something of the message the two writers wanted to get across to their readers.

★ **Poster Poems.** The two posters from the First World War recruiting campaign were attempts by the government of the day to put emotional and moral pressure on the men of Britain to enlist. The hard statistics of the dead and wounded given on page 96 give you some idea of what awaited many of those who joined up. In groups, discuss the message of each poster and the ways in which they work. What do you imagine is going through the minds of the people depicted in each poster? On your own, take either of the two recruiting slogans—'Daddy, what did *YOU* do in the Great War?' or 'Women of Britain say *GO!*'—and use them as the first line of a piece of your own writing.

★ **Performing.** Henry Reed's poem *Naming of Parts* on page 83 is a poem for two voices. The voice of the army Instructor going through the naming of the different parts of the rifle which has just been issued to the new recruits begins each of the first four verses and dominates them. In the final sentence of each of these verses the daydreaming thoughts of the soldier take over replacing the

Instructor's images of death with images of life and love. In the fifth and final verse the soldier-author's voice takes over completely. Read the poem together in pairs trying to capture the bullying voice of the Instructor and the dreamier, wistful tones of the new recruit.

You might like to pair Ted Hughes' *Bayonet Charge* on page 84 with Henry Reed's poem. Here the rifle with its bayonet is not simply a piece of equipment but a violent and deadly weapon in the hands of a terrified and anguished man. With practice a single voice can carry the poem through from start to finish but you might try experimenting with reading it using two voices. There is a moment of stillness lasting from the second line of the second verse to half-way through the last line of that same verse. A quieter, more reflective tone is needed for this central passage.

* **Word Sculpture.** Henry Moore's sculpture, *Atom Piece* on page 93 contains a number of metaphors. What can you see in the shape: a mushroom cloud, a skull, a bomb-casing? What is the effect of the scratched surfaces in the lower part of the sculpture below the contrasting smoothness of the dome? Try to create your own *Atom Piece* in words concentrating on ideas and images suggested by this sculpture. You may find it helpful to focus on a single image or comparison in a haiku or to produce a shape poem where the shape of the words on the page echoes the shape of the sculpture.

* **Discussion.** The poems on pages 88–94 all offer different ways of thinking about the unthinkable. Push-button nuclear warfare, unlike the muddy conflict of the trenches, is inhumanly detached from individuals yet its consequences are unimaginably greater and its aftermath may be terrible for any survivors. James Kirkup, who lives and works in Japan, recalls his feelings on finding himself unexpectedly in the rebuilt city of Hiroshima where the first-ever atomic bomb was dropped. Peter Porter offers us, in the bland tones of a radio announcer, the nightmare of the few minutes warning of nuclear attack. Edwin Muir evokes a future war and an image of salvation. These are poems to discuss in small groups though *Your Attention Please* provides an opportunity for a grimly humorous performance. Choose one of these longer poems, discuss it in your group, deciding what its message is, and then present it to the rest of the class.

# Religious Experience

## Church Going

Once I am sure there's nothing going on
I step inside, letting the door thud shut.
Another church: matting, seats, and stone,
And little books; sprawlings of flowers, cut
For Sunday, brownish now; some brass and stuff
Up at the holy end; the small neat organ;
And a tense, musty, unignorable silence,
Brewed God knows how long. Hatless, I take off
My cycle-clips in awkward reverence,

Move forward, run my hand around the font.
From where I stand, the roof looks almost new—
Cleaned, or restored? Someone would know: I don't.
Mounting the lectern, I peruse a few
Hectoring large-scale verses, and pronounce
"Here endeth" much more loudly than I'd meant.
The echoes snigger briefly. Back at the door
I sign the book, donate an Irish sixpence,
Reflect the place was not worth stopping for.

Yet stop I did: in fact I often do,
And always end much at a loss like this,
Wondering what to look for; wondering, too,
When churches fall completely out of use
What we shall turn them into, if we shall keep
A few cathedrals chronically on show,
Their parchment, plate and pyx in locked cases,
And let the rest rent free to rain and sheep.
Shall we avoid them as unlucky places?

Or, after dark, will dubious women come
To make their children touch a particular stone;
Pick simples for a cancer; or on some
Advised night see walking a dead one?
Power of some sort or other will go on
In games, in riddles, seemingly at random;
But superstition, like belief, must die,
And what remains when disbelief has gone?
Grass, weedy pavements, brambles, buttress, sky,

A shape less recognisable each week,
A purpose more obscure. I wonder who
Will be the last, the very last, to seek
This place for what it was; one of the crew
That tap and jot and know what rood-lofts were?
Some ruin-bibber, randy for antique,
Or Christmas-addict, counting on a whiff
Of gown-and-bands and organ-pipes and myrrh?
Or will he be my representative,

Bored, uninformed, knowing the ghostly silt
Dispersed, yet tending to this cross of ground
Through suburb scrub because it held unspilt
So long and equably what since is found
Only in separation—marriage, and birth,
And death, and thoughts of these—for whom was built
This special shell? For, though I've no idea
What this accoutred frowsty barn is worth,
It pleases me to stand in silence here;

A serious house on serious earth it is,
In whose blent air all our compulsions meet,
Are recognised, and robed as destinies.
And that much never can be obsolete,
Since someone will forever be surprising
A hunger in himself to be more serious,
And gravitating with it to this ground,
Which, he once heard, was proper to grow wise in,
If only that so many dead lie round.

PHILIP LARKIN

# The Collar

I struck the board, and cry'd, No more.
                    I will abroad.
            What? shall I ever sigh and pine?
My lines and life are free; free as the rode,
            Loose as the winde, as large as store.
                    Shall I be still in suit?
            Have I no harvest but a thorn
            To let me bloud, and not restore
            What I have lost with cordiall fruit?
                    Sure there was wine
Before my sighs did drie it: there was corn
            Before my tears did drown it.
        Is the yeare onely lost to me?
            Have I no bayes to crown it?
No flowers, no garlands gay? all blasted?
                    All wasted?
        Not so, my heart: but there is fruit,
                    And thou hast hands.
        Recover all thy sigh-blown age
On double pleasures: leave thy cold dispute
Of what is fit, and not. Forsake thy cage,
                    Thy rope of sands,
Which pettie thoughts have made, and made to thee
            Good cable, to enforce and draw,
                    And be thy law,
        While thou didst wink and wouldst not see,
                    Away; take heed:
                    I will abroad.
Call in thy deaths head there: tie up thy fears.
                    He that forbears
            To suit and serve his need,
                    Deserves his load.
But as I rav'd and grew more fierce and wilde
                    At every word,
        Me thoughts I heard one calling, *Child!*
            And I reply'd, *My Lord*.

GEORGE HERBERT

# What Are They Thinking . . .

What are they thinking, the people in churches,
Closing their eyelids and kneeling to pray,
Touching their faces and sniffing their fingers,
Folding their knuckles one over another?
What are they thinking? Do they remember
*This is the church: and this is the steeple:*
*Open the door: and here are the people?*
Do they still see the parson climbing upstairs,
Opening the window and saying his prayers?
Do they perceive in the pit of their palms
The way of the walls and the spin of the spire,
The turmoil of tombstones tossed in the grass,
Under the yawning billows of yew?
Can they discover, drooping beyond them,
The chestnuts' fountains of flowers and frills,
And the huge fields folded into the hills?

What are they thinking, the sheep on the hills,
Bobbing and bending to nibble the grass,
Kissing the crisp green coat of the combes?
What are they thinking, lying contented
With vacant regard in long rumination?
Do they consider the sky as a cage,
Their fleeces as fetters, their bones as their bonds?
Or do they rejoice at the thyme on their tongues,
The dome of the sky, the slope of the downs,
The village below, the church, and the steeple,
With shepherd and ploughman and parson and people?

And what is he feeling, the lark as he flies,
Does he consider the span of his days,
Does he dissever himself from his spirit,
His flight from his feathers, his song from his singing?
Is he cast down at the thought of his brevity?
Or does he look forward to long immortality?
He stitches the sky with the thread of his breath
To all the bright pattern of living beneath,
To ploughman and shepherd and parson and people,
To the sheep on the hills and the church and the steeple.

BRYAN GUINNESS

# God's Grandeur

The world is charged with the grandeur of God.
   It will flame out, like shining from shook foil;
   It gathers to a greatness, like the ooze of oil
Crushed. Why do men then now not reck his rod?
Generations have trod, have trod, have trod;
   And all is seared with trade; bleared, smeared with toil;
   And wears man's smudge and shares man's smell: the soil
Is bare now, nor can foot feel, being shod.

And for all this, nature is never spent;
   There lives the dearest freshness deep down things;
And though the last lights off the black West went
   Oh, morning, at the brown brink eastward, springs—
Because the Holy Ghost over the bent
   World broods with warm breast and with ah! bright wings.

GERARD MANLEY HOPKINS

# A Hymne to God the Father

Wilt thou forgive that sinne where I begunne,
   Which is my sin, though it were done before?
Wilt thou forgive those sinnes through which I runne,
   And do run still: though still I do deplore?
   When thou hast done, thou hast not done,
         For, I have more.

Wilt thou forgive that sinne by which I wonne
   Others to sinne? and, made my sinne their doore?
Wilt thou forgive that sinne which I did shunne
   A yeare, or two: but wallowed in, a score?
   When thou hast done, thou hast not done,
         For, I have more.

104

I have a sinne of feare, that when I have spunne
   My last thred, I shall perish on the shore;
Sweare by thy selfe, that at my death thy Sunne
   Shall shine as he shines now, and heretofore;
   And, having done that, Thou hast done,
        I feare no more.

JOHN DONNE

# Jigsaws V

Although we say we disbelieve,
God comes in handy when we swear—
It may be when we exult or grieve,
It may be just to clear the air;
Let the skew runner breast the tape,
Let the great lion leave his lair,
Let the hot nymph solicit rape,
We need a God to phrase it fair;
When death curls over in the wave
Strings may soar and brass may blare
But, to be frightened or be brave,
We crave some emblem for despair,
And when ice burns and joys are pain
And shadows grasp us by the hair
We need one Name to take in vain,
One taboo to break, one sin to dare.
What is it then we disbelieve?
Because the facts are far from bare
And all religions must deceive
And every proof must wear and tear,
That God exists we cannot show,
So do not know but need not care.
Thank God we do not know; we know
We need the unknown. The Unknown is There.

LOUIS MACNEICE

# Sometime During Eternity

Sometime during eternity
                          some guys show up
and one of them
                  who shows up real late
                                  is a kind of carpenter
from some square-type place
                          like Galilee
    and he starts wailing
                  and claiming he is hip
      to who made heaven
                      and earth
                      and that the cat
        who really laid it on us
                      is his Dad
And moreover
  he adds
          It's all writ down
                          on some scroll-type parchments
      which some henchmen
            leave lying around the Dead Sea somewheres
            a long time ago
                      and which you won't even find
for a coupla thousand years or so
                              or at least for
      nineteen hundred and fortyseven
                              of them
              to be exact
                      and even then
      nobody really believes them
                      or me
                              for that matter
        You're hot
        they tell him
        And they cool him
        They stretch him on the Tree to cool
            And everybody after that
                              is always making models
            of this Tree
                      with Him hung up

and always crooning his name
                              and calling Him to come down
                and sit in
                          on their combo
              as if he is *the* king cat
                              who's got to blow
        or they can't quite make it
        Only he don't come down
                              from His Tree
    Him just hang there
                      on His Tree
                              looking real Petered out
                and real cool
                              and also
        according to a roundup
                          of late world news
      from the usual unreliable sources
                              real dead.

LAWRENCE FERLINGHETTI

# The Killing

That was the day they killed the Son of God
On a squat hill-top by Jerusalem.
Zion was bare, her children from their maze
Sucked by the demon curiosity
Clean through the gates. The very halt and blind
Had somehow got themselves up to the hill.

After the ceremonial preparation,
The scourging, nailing, nailing against the wood,
Erection of the main-trees with their burden,
While from the hill rose an orchestral wailing,
They were there at last, high up in the soft spring day.
We watched the writhings, heard the moanings, saw
The three heads turning on their separate axles
Like broken wheels left spinning. Round *his* head
Was loosely bound a crown of plaited thorn
That hurt at random, stinging temple and brow
As the pain swung into its envious circle.
In front the wreath was gathered in a knot
That as he gazed looked like the last stump left
Of a death-wounded deer's great antlers. Some
Who came to stare grew silent as they looked,
Indignant or sorry. But the hardened old
And the hard-hearted young, although at odds
From the first morning, cursed him with one curse,
Having prayed for a Rabbi or an armed Messiah
And found the Son of God. What use to them
Was a God or a Son of God? Of what avail
For purposes such as theirs? Beside the cross-foot,
Alone, four women stood and did not move
All day. The sun revolved, the shadow wheeled,
The evening fell. His head lay on his breast,
But in his breast they watched his heart move on
By itself alone, accomplishing its journey.
Their taunts grew louder, sharpened by the knowledge
That he was walking in the park of death,
Far from their rage. Yet all grew stale at last,
Spite, curiosity, envy, hate itself.
They waited only for death and death was slow
And came so quietly they scarce could mark it.
They were angry then with death and death's deceit.

I was a stranger, could not read these people
Or this outlandish deity. Did a God
Indeed in dying cross my life that day
By chance, he on his road and I on mine?

EDWIN MUIR

The poems in this section show many different attitudes towards religious experience. Although they often reflect specifically Christian concerns, the questions they address are relevant to anyone who thinks about religion, from whatever standpoint. Some of you may have felt drawn to the agnosticism of Philip Larkin's poem *Church Going* (p. 99), others to the unspecified but necessary God of Louis Macneice's *Jigsaws V* (p. 105) and feel like him that 'we know / We need the unknown'. Some of you may respond to the questioning restlessness of Herbert's poem *The Collar* (p. 101); others again to the exulting praise and worship of Hopkins' *God's Grandeur* (p. 104). Before you go further it is worth discussing two questions:

—Do you feel you must share the religious attitude or belief expressed in a poem in order to be able to *enjoy* that poem?

—If you find yourself out of sympathy with what a poem says, does this prevent you from *appreciating* the poem as a piece of writing? When you have read and discussed several of the poems in this section come back to those same questions again.

★ **Three Poems by three priests.** Not immediately perhaps the most exciting thought, but these three poems are full of their own human drama and reflect the struggles and conflicts of three men who had chosen to serve their God as priests yet suffered the doubts and weaknesses shared by all of us.

In small groups try to decide how these three poems might be read and, if you feel sufficiently confident, try to link them as a performance. They were all of them written at least a hundred years ago so the language might give you some problems at first but you will find they repay study. Here are some thoughts to start you off:

—The 'collar' of George Herbert's poem on page 101 is the 'dog-collar' worn by priests and the 'board' that he strikes in his anger is the altar—the Lord's Table. Herbert came from a very wealthy and powerful family and was known at Court where his brother, Lord Herbert, was a distinguished diplomat. George chose, after some struggle, to become a simple parish priest ministering to ordinary people and dedicated himself to the task. Nonetheless he sometimes had to wrestle with a part of himself that wanted to be free and to lead a life of pleasure and luxury. The irregular pattern of lines indicates something of the writer's turbulent emotional state. Look how it ranges and rages across the page always questioning and exclaiming against being 'in suit' to—that is, 'under contract to serve'—God. It's a dramatic piece and needs careful preparation before reading, but it's worth the effort for it takes us, even 350 years later, to the heart of one man's spiritual struggle. Does the 'Child' at the end refer to the childish anger he has poured out or to his relationship with God . . . or both?

—John Donne was also a priest and a contemporary of George Herbert. Before becoming a priest he had been a soldier, diplomat, courtier and writer of love poetry. It is perhaps something of this past life he remembers in his *Hymne to God the Father* (p. 104) which was probably written during his illness of 1623—an illness from which he did not expect to recover. The poem depends upon a clever play on words for the poet's own name was pronounced 'done'. Thus, 'When thou hast done thou hast not done' uses the word in both senses ('thou hast not Donne'). Is there another similar pun in the last verse?

—*God's Grandeur* (p. 104) by a Roman Catholic priest, Gerard Manley Hopkins, is a sonnet which celebrates his belief in God's and Nature's power to care for and to restore humanity despite its faults. It too has an anguished question at its heart—'Why do men then now not reck his rod?' that is: 'Why doesn't mankind obey God's law any longer?'

All three poems hinge on questions and have an element of doubt and turmoil but all end on a positive note of resolution and faith.

★ **Performing.** Read Lawrence Ferlinghetti's poem *Sometime During Eternity*. Although it is closer to us in time than any of the three poems mentioned above, it is in some ways curiously more dated with its 1960s Beat generation images and language. Try to capture the 'cool', 'hip', 'laid back' style in a group reading; the poem might go well split between four voices.

★ **Performing and Writing.** In groups plan a reading of Bryan Guinness's poem *What Are they Thinking . . .* As you will see, he uses a children's rhyme at the heart of his poem: *'This is the church: and this is the steeple: Open the door: and here are the people'.* Do any of you remember the actions that accompany the rhyme? The poem can be read by three voices each taking one of the main sections or it can be split into smaller units if you wish.

What *are* they thinking, these people in churches: as they pray, as they listen to the sermon, as they sing? Perhaps you could write a poem that answers the question by trying to enter the minds of various members of the congregation. Concentrate on two or three in your mind's eye—elderly folk, the very young, the businessman, the teenagers perhaps . . . What *are* they thinking?

* **Picture into Poem.** It is worth asking yourself not only what the people are thinking but also what goes on in the mind of the central figure in a religious service. The photograph on page 103 shows three Italian priests at midnight mass. Look carefully at the picture and at the faces of the three men. How do they appear to you? What are *they* thinking? You may have the basis for a piece of original writing here.

* **Looking and Seeing.** Many writers have felt that if they could fully understand what are apparently the simplest things—a flower, a grain of sand, a butterfly's wing—they would understand the central mysteries of life and the universe. And whilst we might in our wisdom talk knowledgeably about evolution they are, whatever our views, quite amazing things. Do any things that we take for granted seem to you similarly remarkable? In pairs, jot down two or three ideas and share them. There may be the basis for a poem here.

# Satire and Protest

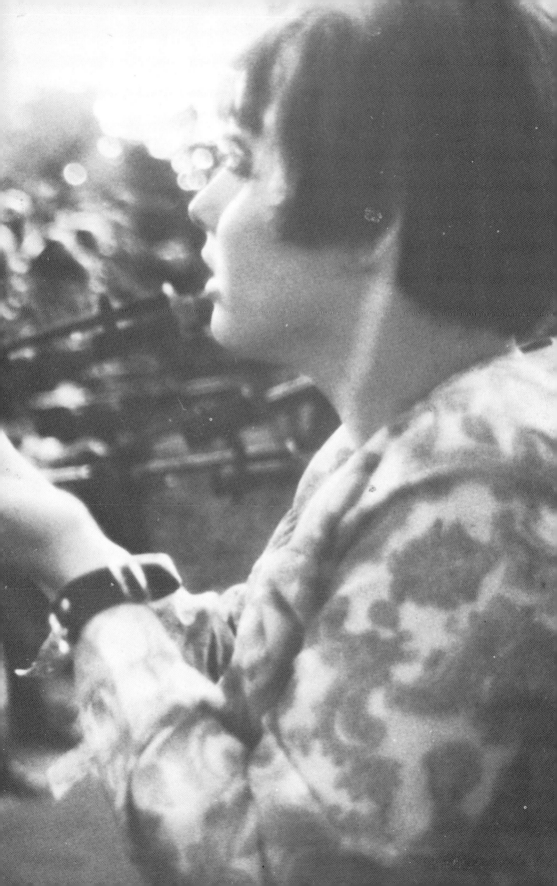

# Lies

Telling lies to the young is wrong.
Proving to them that lies are true is wrong.
Telling them that God's in his heaven
and all's well with the world is wrong.
The young know what you mean. The young are people.
Tell them the difficulties can't be counted,
and let them see not only what will be
but see with clarity these present times.
Say obstacles exist they must encounter
sorrow happens, hardship happens.
The hell with it. Who never knew
the price of happiness will not be happy.
Forgive no error you recognise,
it will repeat itself, increase,
and afterwards our pupils
will not forgive in us what we forgave.

Y. YEVTUSHENKO
*(trans. R. Milner-Gulland and P. Levi, S.J.)*

# Prayer of a Black Boy

Lord, I am so tired.
Tired I entered this world.
Far have I wandered since the cock crew,
And the road to school is steep.
Lord, I do not want to go into their school,
Please help me that I need not go again.
I want to follow father into the cool gorges.
When the night is hovering over magic forests
Where spirits play before dawn.
Barefoot, I want to tread the red-hot paths,
That boil in midday sun.
And then lie down to sleep beneath a Mango tree.

And I want to wake up only
When down there the white man's siren starts to howl,
And the factory,
A ship on the sugarfields,
Lands and spits its crew
Of black workers into the landscape . . .
Lord, I do not want to go into their school,
Please help me that I need not go again,
It's true, they say a little negro ought to go,
So that he might become
Just like the gentlemen of the city,
So that he might become a real gentleman.
But I, I do not want to become
A gentleman of the city, or as they call it
A real gentleman.
I'd rather stroll along the sugar stores
Where the tight sacks are piled
With brown sugar, brown like my skin.
I'd rather listen—when the moon is whispering
Tenderly into the ear of cocopalms,
To what the old man who always smokes
Recites with breaking voice during the night,
The stories of Samba and Master Hare
And many others more that are not found in any book.
Lord, the negroes have had too much work already,
Why should we learn again from foreign books,
About all kinds of things we've never seen?
And then, their school is far too sad,
Just as sad as these gentlemen of the city,
These real gentlemen
Who do not even know how to dance by the light of the moon,
Who do not even know how to walk on the flesh of their feet,
Who do not even know how to tell the tales of their fathers
By the light of their nightly fires.
O Lord, I do not want to go into their schools again.

GUY TIROLIEN

# Telephone Conversation

The price seemed reasonable, location
Indifferent. The landlady swore she lived
Off premises. Nothing remained
But self-confession. 'Madam,' I warned,
'I hate a wasted journey—I am African.'
Silence. Silenced transmission of
Pressurized good-breeding. Voice, when it came,
Lipstick coated, long gold-rolled
Cigarette-holder pipped. Caught I was, foully.
'HOW DARK?' . . . I had not misheard . . . 'ARE YOU LIGHT
OR VERY DARK?' Button B. Button A. Stench
Of rancid breath of public hide-and-speak.
Red booth. Red pillar-box. Red double-tiered
Omnibus squelching tar. It *was* real! Shamed
By ill-mannered silence, surrender
Pushed dumbfounded to beg simplification.
Considerate she was, varying the emphasis—
'ARE YOU DARK? OR VERY LIGHT?' Revelation came.
'You mean—like plain or milk chocolate?'
Her assent was clinical, crushing in its light
Impersonality. Rapidly, wave-length adjusted,
I chose. 'West African sepia'—and as afterthought,
'Down in my passport.' Silence for spectroscopic
Flight of fancy, till truthfulness clanged her accent
Hard on the mouthpiece. 'WHAT'S THAT?' conceding
'DON'T KNOW WHAT THAT IS.' 'Like brunette.'
'THAT'S DARK, ISN'T IT?' 'Not altogether.
Facially, I am brunette, but madam, you should see
The rest of me. Palm of my hand, soles of my feet
Are a peroxide blonde. Friction, caused—
Foolishly madam—by sitting down, has turned
My bottom raven black—One moment madam!'—sensing
Her receiver rearing on the thunderclap
About my ears—'Madam,' I pleaded, 'wouldn't you rather
See for yourself?'

WOLE SOYINKA

116

# Remember?

Remember me?
I am the girl
with the dark skin
whose shoes are thin
I am the girl
with rotted teeth
I am the dark
rotten-toothed girl
with the wounded eye
and the melted ear.

I am the girl
holding their babies
cooking their meals
sweeping their yards
washing their clothes
Dark and rotting
and wounded, wounded.

I would give
to the human race
only hope.

I am the woman
with the blessed
dark skin
I am the woman
with teeth repaired
I am the woman
with the healing eye
the ear that hears.

I am the woman: Dark,
repaired, healed
Listening to you.

I would give
to the human race
only hope.

I am the woman
offering two flowers
whose roots
are twin

Justice and Hope

Let us begin.

ALICE WALKER

# ygUDuh

ygUDuh

ydoan
yunnuhstan

ydoan o
yunnuhstan dem
yguduh ged

yunnuhstan dem doidee
yguduh ged riduh
ydoan o nudn
LISN bud LISN

dem
gud
am

lidl yelluh bas
tuds weer goin

duhSIVILEYEzum

e. e. cummings

# Refugee Blues

Say this city has ten million souls,
Some are living in mansions, some are living in holes:
Yet there's no place for us, my dear, yet there's no place for us.

Once we had a country and we thought it fair,
Look in the atlas and you'll find it there:
We cannot go there now, my dear, we cannot go there now.

In the village churchyard there grows an old yew,
Every spring it blossoms anew:
Old passports can't do that, my dear, old passports can't do that.

The consul banged the table and said:
'If you've got no passport you're officially dead':
But we are still alive, my dear, but we are still alive.

Went to a committee; they offered me a chair;
Asked me politely to return next year:
But where shall we go today, my dear, but where shall we go
    today?

Came to a public meeting; the speaker got up and said:
'If we let them in, they will steal our daily bread';
He was talking of you and me, my dear, he was talking of you
    and me.

Thought I heard the thunder rumbling in the sky;
It was Hitler over Europe, saying: 'They must die';
O we were in his mind, my dear, O we were in his mind.

Saw a poodle in a jacket fastened with a pin,
Saw a door opened and a cat let in:
But they weren't German Jews, my dear, but they weren't
    German Jews.

Went down to the harbour and stood upon the quay,
Saw the fish swimming as if they were free:
Only ten feet away, my dear, only ten feet away.

Walked through a wood, saw the birds in the trees;
They had no politicians and sang at their ease:
They weren't the human race, my dear, they weren't the human
 race.

Dreamed I saw a building with a thousand floors,
A thousand windows and a thousand doors;
Not one of them was ours, my dears, not one of them was ours.

Stood on a great plain in the falling snow;
Ten thousand soldiers marched to and fro:
Looking for you and me, my dear, looking for you and me.

W. H. AUDEN

# The Unknown Citizen

He was found by the Bureau of Statistics to be
One against whom there was no official complaint,
And all the reports on his conduct agree
That, in the modern sense of an old-fashioned word, he was
    a saint,
For in everything he did he served the Greater Community.
Except for the war till the day he retired
He worked in a factory and never got fired,
But satisfied his employers, Fudge Motors Inc.,
Yet he wasn't a scab or odd in his views,
For his Union reports that he paid his dues,
(Our report on his Union shows it was sound)
And our Social Psychology workers found
That he was popular with his mates and liked a drink.
The Press are convinced that he bought a paper every day
And that his reactions to advertisements were normal in every
    way.
Policies taken out in his name prove that he was fully insured,
And his Health-card shows he was once in hospital but left it
    cured.
Both Producers Research and High-Grade Living declare
He was fully sensible to the advantages of the Instalment Plan
And had everything necessary to the Modern Man,
A phonograph, a radio, a car and a frigidaire.
Our researchers into Public Opinion are content
That he held the proper opinions for the time of year;
When there was peace, he was for peace; when there was war,
    he went.
He was married and added five children to the population,
Which our Eugenist says was the right number for a parent of
    his generation,
And our teachers report that he never interfered with their
    education.
Was he free? Was he happy? The question is absurd;
Had anything been wrong, we should certainly have heard.

W. H. AUDEN

# Algerian Refugee Camp Aïn-Khemouda

You have black eyes,
Four years of age,
A chic, cast-off coat
—pepper-and-salt, double-breasted—
A label naming you 'Mohammed',
Some slippers, a squashed felt hat.
Nothing else. And 'nothing' means just that.

This camp is your home until—well, until.
A flag flaps on a hill.
The *oued* soon will be dry;
Do you know how to cry?

Smoke curls from the tents
Where women who are not your mother,
Hennaed and trinketed, cook.
Your eyes see but do not look.
And men who are not your father,
Turbaned and burned, sit stiff
In rows, like clay pigeons, on a cliff.
Targets do not easily relax.
Your hair is fair as flax.

Guns rattle the mauve hills
Where the last warmth spills
On villages where once you were
One of a family that died.
Not much else. Just that.

You pull down the brim of your hat.
Who knows what goes on inside?

ALAN ROSS

# A Beautiful Young Nymph Going to Bed

*Written for the honour of the fair sex*

Corinna, pride of Drury-lane,
For whom no shepherd sighs in vain;
Never did Covent-Garden boast
So bright a batter'd strolling toast!
No drunken rake to pick her up;
No cellar where on tick to sup;
Returning at the midnight hour,
Four stories climbing to her bower;
Then, seated on a three-legg'd chair,
Takes off her artificial hair;
Now picking out a crystal eye,
She wipes it clean and lays it by.
Her eyebrows from a mouse's hide
Stuck on with art on either side,
Pulls off with care, and first displays 'em,
Then in a play-book smoothly lays 'em,
Now dextrously her plumpers draws,
That serve to fill her hollow jaws,
Untwists a wire, and from her gums
A set of teeth completely comes;
Proceeding on, the lovely goddess
Unlaces next her steel-ribb'd bodice,
Which, by the operator's skill,
Press down the lumps, the hollows fill.
Up goes her hand and off she slips
The bolsters that supply her hips.
But must, before she goes to bed,
Rub off the daubs of white and red,
And smooth the furrows in her front
With greasy paper stuck upon't.
She takes a bolus[1] ere she sleeps;
And then between two blankets creeps.

JONATHAN SWIFT

[1] a large pill

124

# Geriatric Ward

Feeding time in the geriatric ward;
I wondered how they found their mouths,
and seeing that not one looked up, inquired
'Do they have souls?'

'If I had a machine-gun,' answered the doctor
'I'd show you dignity in death instead of living death.
Death wasn't meant to be kept alive.
But we're under orders
to pump blood and air in after the mind's gone.
I don't understand souls;
I only learned about cells
law-abiding as leaves
withering under frost.
But we, never handing over
to Mother who knows best,
spray cabbages with oxygen, hoping for a smile,
count pulses of breathing bags whose direction is lost,
and think we've won.

Here's a game you can't win—
One by one they ooze away in the cold.
There's no society forbidding
this dragged-out detention of the old.'

PHOEBE HESKETH

125

# How Beastly the Bourgeois Is

How beastly the bourgeois is
especially the male of the species—

Presentable eminently presentable—
shall I make you a present of him?

Isn't he handsome? isn't he healthy? Isn't he a fine specimen?
doesn't he look the fresh clean englishman, outside?
Isn't it god's own image? tramping his thirty miles a day
after partridges, or a little rubber ball?
wouldn't you like to be like that, well off, and quite the thing?

Oh, but wait!
Let him meet a new emotion, let him be faced with another
    man's need,
Let him come home to a bit of moral difficulty, let life face him
    with a new demand on his understanding
and then watch him go soggy, like a wet meringue.
Watch him turn into a mess, either a fool or a bully.
Just watch the display of him, confronted with a new demand
    on his intelligence,
a new life-demand.

How beastly the bourgeois is
especially the male of the species—

Nicely groomed, like a mushroom
standing there so sleek and erect and eyeable—
and like a fungus, living on the remains of bygone life
sucking his life out of the dead leaves of greater life than
    his own.

And even so, he's stale, he's been there too long.
Touch him, and you'll find he's all gone inside
just like an old mushroom, all wormy inside, and hollow
under a smooth skin and an upright appearance.
Full of seething, wormy, hollow feelings
rather nasty—
How beastly the bourgeois is!

Standing in their thousands, these appearances, in damp
  England
what a pity they can't all be kicked over
like sickening toadstools, and left to melt back, swiftly
into the soil of England.

D. H. LAWRENCE

## 'They'

The Bishop tell us: 'When the boys come back
'They will not be the same; for they'll have fought
'In a just cause: they lead the last attack
'On Anti-Christ; their comrades' blood has bought
'New right to breed an honourable race,
'They have challenged Death and dared him face to face.'

'We're none of us the same!' the boys reply.
'For George lost both his legs; and Bill's stone blind;
'Poor Jim's shot through the lungs and like to die;
'And Bert's gone syphilitic: you'll not find
'A chap who's served that hasn't found *some* change.'
And the Bishop said: 'The ways of God are strange!'

SIEGFRIED SASSOON

## Base Details

If I were fierce, and bald, and short of breath,
    I'd live with scarlet Majors at the Base,
And speed glum heroes up the line to death.
    You'd see me with my puffy petulant face,
Guzzling and gulping in the best hotel,
    Reading the Roll of Honour. 'Poor young chap,'
I'd say—'I used to know his father well;
    Yes, we've lost heavily in this last scrap.'
And when the war is done and youth stone dead,
I'd toddle safely home and die—in bed.

SIEGFRIED SASSOON

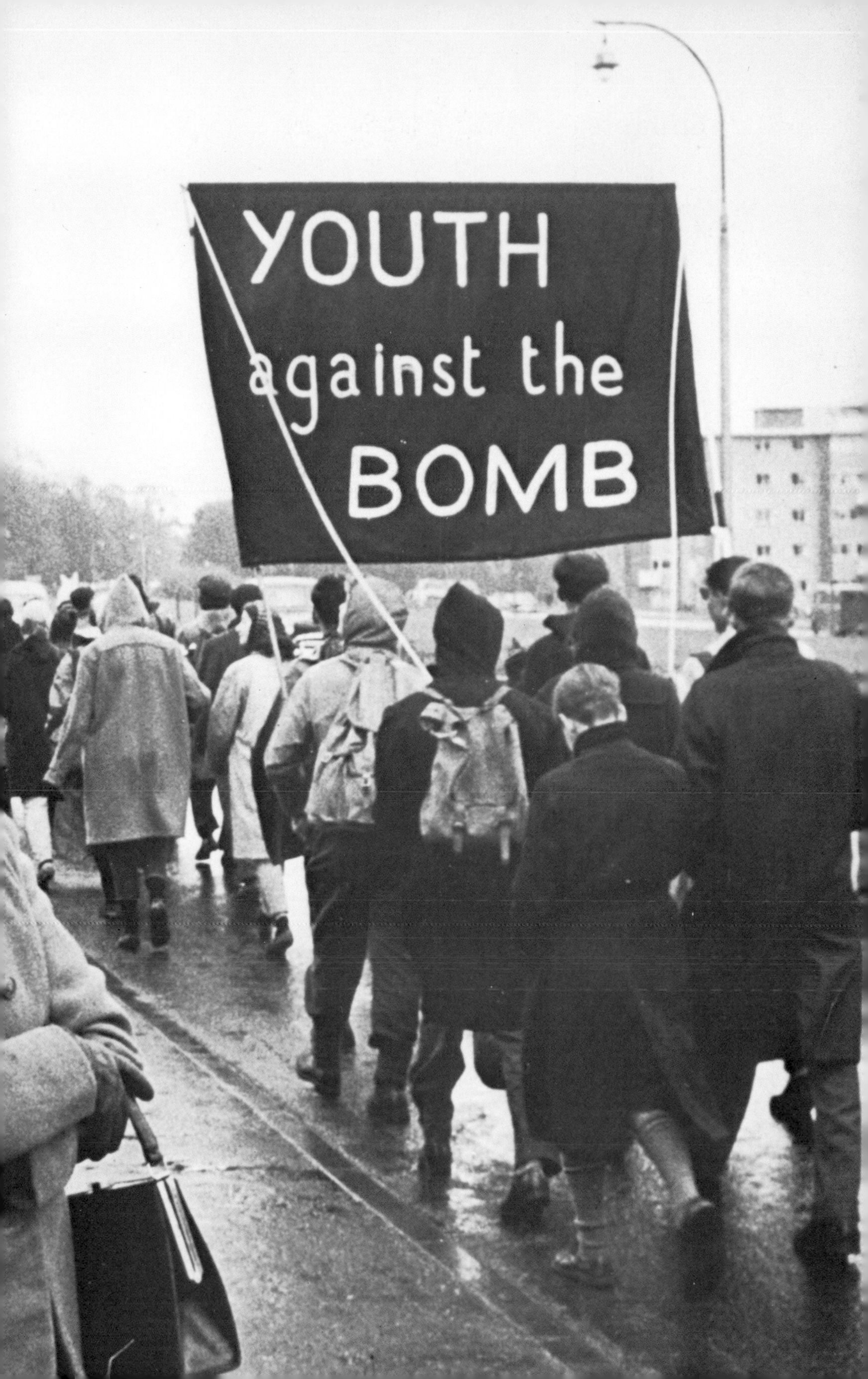
YOUTH
against the
BOMB

# Epitaph

They hanged him on a clement morning, swung
between the falling sunlight and the women's
breathing, like a black apostrophe to pain.
All morning, while the children hushed
their hop-scotch joy and the cane kept growing,
he hung there, sweet and low.

                          At least, that's how
they tell it. It was long ago.
And what can we recall of a dead slave or two,
except that, when we punctuate our island tale,
they swing like sighs across the brutal
sentences, and anger pauses
till they pass away.

DENNIS SCOTT

# Strange Fruit

*As sung by Billie Holiday on 'Lady Sings the Blues', Verve 3113–109 (Polydor)*

Southern trees bear a strange fruit,
Blood on the leaves and blood at the root,
Black bodies swinging in the southern breeze,
Strange fruit hanging from the poplar trees.
Pastoral scene of the gallant south,
The bulging eyes and the twisted mouth,
Scent of magnolia, sweet and fresh
Then the sudden smell of burning flesh.
Here is a fruit for the crows to pluck,
For the rain together, for the wind to suck,
For the sun to rot, for the trees to drop,
Here is a strange and bitter crop.

LEWIS ALLAN

# Ku Klux

They took me out
To some lonesome place.
They said, 'Do you believe
In the great white race?'

I said, 'Mister,
To tell you the truth,
I'd believe in anything
If you'd just turn me loose.'

The white man said, 'Boy
Can it be
You're a-standin' there
A-sassin' me?'

They hit me in the head
And knocked me down.
And then they kicked me
On the ground.

A klansman said, 'Nigger,
Look me in the face—
And tell me you believe in
The great white race.'

LANGSTON HUGHES

# Epitaph On A Dead Statesman

I could not dig: I dared not rob:
Therefore I lied to please the mob.
Now all my lies are proved untrue
And I must face the men I slew.
What tale shall serve me here among
Mine angry and defrauded young?

RUDYARD KIPLING

# A Protest in the Sixth Year of Ch'ien Fu (AD 879)

The hills and rivers of the lowland country
    You have made your battle-ground.
How do you suppose the people who live there
    Will procure 'firewood and hay'?[1]
Do not let me hear you talking together
    About titles and promotions;
For a single general's reputation
    Is made out of ten thousand corpses.

TS'AO SUNG
(trans. Arthur Waley)

[1] the necessities of life

This section consists of satires and protests against aspects of life that different writers have felt bound to bring to our notice. A satire is a poem which sets out to ridicule what the writer sees as the vices or follies of the age. It is a way of making a protest. Some of the poems are concerned with trivial and irksome things that irritate and even amuse the writer; some go much deeper and are born of deep anger and despair at human stupidity.

* **Reading and Performance.** The poems on pages 114–18 and 130–1 all deal with aspects of racial prejudice and, in the case of the Lewis Allan song, with the horrific murders of blacks by whites in the American Deep South. Such evil perhaps finds its beginnings in what may at first seem relatively minor pieces of small-minded thinking such as that encountered by the black African poet, Wole Soyinka, when he came to England to study as a young man, some twenty-five years before he was awarded the Nobel Prize for Literature (p. 116). He recounts his experience of telephoning a white landlady to arrange accommodation. In pairs read the poem as a dialogue. Try to capture the changing tones of voice as each speaker begins to realise what the situation is.

* **Couplets.** Pretence, hypocrisy, vanity, pride, people affecting to be what they are not are common objects of the satirist's mockery. Swift's rather cruel caricature of the 'Beautiful Young Nymph' undressing for bed was written well over two hundred and fifty years ago. It is deliberately exaggerated and gains much of its life from the rhymed couplets—pairs of rhymed lines—that Swift uses. Listen carefully to the rhythm of the lines and then, with your pen dipped in acid, try to create rhymed couplets of your own to describe your chosen target.

* **Performing.** Siegfried Sassoon's poems on page 127, like those in the *War* section of this book, are powerful protests against those who stayed safe whilst sending thousands of young men to their deaths. Both poems can be read aloud by two or more voices. In small groups arrange a reading that brings out the full force of Sassoon's bitter anger.
—If you feel like taking up a real challenge, try reading e. e. cummings' poem *ygUDuh* aloud (p. 119). It too is a protest poem about attitudes to war—the Vietnam war this time. It may take you one or two tries to sort it out. The solution is to get the accent right and to *listen* to it!

* **Refugee Blues.** W. H. Auden's two poems about refugees (pp. 120–122) were written when Hitler was destroying the lives of

133

millions of people across Europe. Homeless and stateless, the survivors wandered with their few possessions seeking those who would take them in. Half a century on the world still has its dispossessed. Working in groups, arrange a reading of the two poems using several people's voices. Try to catch the sad refrain of *Refugee Blues* and the tones of cold impersonality in *The Unknown Citizen*.

★ **Poems and Pictures.** The photograph on page 128 shows a protest in two directions: the onlookers seem not to approve of the protesters. The photograph on page 112 shows a direct confrontation of a young woman with equally young guardsmen as she tries to make a peaceful protest. Look carefully at each of these pictures and, if you feel one of them suggests an idea for a piece of writing, focus your attention on it and quickly jot down your thoughts and feelings to work up into a poem later.

—What is Bruno Paul attacking in his satirical cartoon of the two soldiers below? Can you use his picture as a starting point for a piece of your own writing?

*Above the uniform is situated a head for the soldier to know how high the hand has to be lifted to make a salute*

# Family

## Morning Song

Love set you going like a fat gold watch.
The midwife slapped your footsoles, and your bald cry
Took its place among the elements.

Our voices echo, magnifying your arrival. New statue.
In a drafty museum, your nakedness
Shadows our safety. We stand round blankly as walls.

I'm no more your mother
Than the cloud that distils a mirror to reflect its own slow
Effacement at the wind's hand.

All night your moth-breath
Flickers among the flat pink roses. I wake to listen:
A far sea moves in my ear.

One cry, and I stumble from bed, cow-heavy and floral
In my Victorian nightgown.
Your mouth opens clean as a cat's. The window square

Whitens and swallows its dull stars. And now you try
Your handful of notes;
The clear vowels rise like balloons.

SYLVIA PLATH

# Baby Running Barefoot

When the white feet of the baby beat across the grass
The little white feet nod like white flowers in a wind,
They poise and run like puffs of wind that pass
Over water where the weeds are thinned.

And the sight of their white playing in the grass
Is winsome as a robin's song, so fluttering:
Or like two butterflies that settle on a glass
Cup for a moment, soft little wing-beats uttering.

And I wish that the baby would tack across here to me
Like a wind-shadow running on a pond, so she could stand
With two little bare white feet upon my knee
And I could feel her feet in either hand

Cool as syringa buds in morning hours,
Or firm and silken as young peony flowers.          D. H. LAWRENCE

# A Child Half-asleep

Stealthily parting the small-hours silence,
a hardly-embodied figment of his brain
comes down to sit with me
as I work late.
Flat-footed, as though his legs and feet
were still asleep.

On a stool,
staring into the fire,
his dummy dangling.

Fire ignites the small coals of his eyes:
it stares back through the holes
into his head, into the darkness.

I ask what woke him.

'A wolf dreamed me,' he says.                TONY CONNOR

# The Almond Tree

I

All the way to the hospital
the lights were green as peppermints.
Trees of black iron broke into leaf
ahead of me, as if
I were the lucky prince
in an enchanted wood
summoning summer with my whistle,
banishing winter with a nod.

Swung by the road from bend to bend,
I was aware that blood was running
down through the delta of my wrist
and under arches
of bright bone. Centuries,
continents it had crossed;
from an undisclosed beginning
spiralling to an unmapped end.

II

Crossing (at sixty) Magdalen Bridge
*Let it be a son, a son,* said
the man in the driving mirror,
*Let it be a son.* The tower
held up its hand: the college
bells shook their blessing on his head.

III

I parked in an almond's
shadow blossom, for the tree
was waving, waving me
upstairs with a child's hands.

IV

Up
the spinal stair
and at the top

along
a bone-white corridor
the blood tide swung
me swung me to a room
whose walls shuddered
with the shuddering womb.
Under the sheet
wave after wave, wave
after wave beat
on the bone coast, bringing
ashore—whom?
                    New—
minted, my bright farthing!
Coined by our love, stamped with
our images, how you
enrich us! Both
you make one. Welcome
to your white sheet,
my best poem!

V

At seven-thirty
the visitors' bell
scissored the calm
of the corridors.
The doctor walked with me
to the slicing doors.
His hand upon my arm,
his voice—*I have to tell
you*—set another bell
beating in my head:
*your son is a mongol*
the doctor said.

VI

How easily the word went in—
clean as a bullet
leaving no mark on the skin,
stopping the heart within it.

This was my first death.
The 'I' ascending on a slow
last thermal breath
studied the man below
as a pilot treading air might
the buckled shell of his plane—
boot, glove, and helmet
feeling no pain

from the snapped wires' radiant ends.
Looking down from a thousand feet
I held four walls in the lens
of an eye; wall, window, the street

a torrent of windscreens, my own
car under its almond tree,
and the almond waving me down.
I wrestled against gravity,

but light was melting and the gulf
cracked open. Unfamiliar
the body of my late self
I carried to the car.


VII

The hospital—its heavy freight
lashed down ship-shape ward over ward—
steamed into night with some on board
soon to be lost if the desperate

charts were known. Others would come
altered to land or find the land
altered. At their voyage's end
some would be added to, some

diminished. In a numbered cot
my son sailed from me: never to come
ashore into my kingdom
speaking my language. Better not

look that way. The almond tree
was beautiful in labour. Blood—
dark, quickening, bud after bud
split, flower after flower shook free.

On the darkening wind a pale
face floated. Out of reach. Only when
the buds, all the buds, were broken
would the tree be in full sail.

In labour the tree was becoming
itself. I, too, rooted in earth
and ringed by darkness, from the death
of myself saw myself blossoming,

wrenched from the caul of my thirty
years' growing, fathered by my son,
unkindly in a kind season
by love shattered and set free.

VIII

You turn to the window for the first time.
I am called to the cot
to see your focus shift,
take tendril-hold on a shaft
of sun, explore its dusty surface, climb
to an eye you cannot

meet. You have a sickness they cannot heal
the doctors say: locked in
your body you will remain.
Well, I have been locked in mine.
We will tunnel each other out. You seal
the covenant with a grin.

In the days we have known one another,
my little mongol love,
I have learnt more from your lips
than you will from mine perhaps:
I have learnt that to live is to suffer,
to suffer is to live.                                    JON STALLWORTHY

141

# Death of a Son

(who died in a mental hospital, aged one)

Something has ceased to come along with me.
Something like a person: something very like one.
    And there was no nobility in it
        Or anything like that.

Something was there like a one-year-
Old house, dumb as stone. While the near buildings
    Sang like birds and laughed
        Understanding the pact

They were to have with silence. But he
Neither sang nor laughed. He did not bless silence
    Like bread, with words.
        He did not forsake silence.

But rather, like a house in mourning
Kept the eye turned to watch the silence while
    The other houses like birds
        Sang around him.

And the breathing silence neither
Moved nor was still.

I have seen stones: I have seen brick
But this house was made up of neither bricks nor stone
    But a house of flesh and blood
        With flesh of stone

And bricks for blood. A house
Of stones and blood in breathing silence with the other
    Birds singing crazy on its chimneys.
        But this was silence,

This was something else, this was
Hearing and speaking though he was a house drawn
    Into silence, this was
        Something religious in his silence,

Something shining in his quiet,
This was different this was altogether something else:
    Though he never spoke, this
        Was something to do with death.

And then slowly the eye stopped looking
Inward. The silence rose and became still.
The look turned to the outer place and stopped,
    With the birds still shrilling around him.
        And as if he could speak

He turned over on his side with this one year
Red as a wound
He turned over as if he could be sorry for this
And out of his eyes two great tears rolled, like stones,
                and he died.

JON SILKIN

# For My Son

    Not ever to talk when merely requested,
    Not ever to be the performing child,
    This is what you would establish;
                    always keeping
    Private and awkward counsel against
    All coaxing; and going—one hopes—
    The way of a good will,

    To your own true designs. Which is
    The way of some human institutions,
    Growing not as any collective urge
                    would have them
    (In its own placable image) but into
    Their own more wayward value—strong,
    Untidy, original, self-possessed.

ALAN BROWNJOHN

# Afternoons

Summer is fading:
The leaves fall in ones and twos
From trees bordering
The new recreation ground.
In the hollows of afternoons
Young mothers assemble
At swing and sandpit
Setting free their children.

Behind them, at intervals,
Stand husbands in skilled trades,
An estateful of washing,
And the albums, lettered
*Our Wedding*, lying
Near the television:
Before them, the wind
Is ruining their courting-places

That are still courting-places
(but the lovers are all in school),
And their children, so intent on
Finding more unripe acorns,
Expect to bc taken home.
Their beauty has thickened.
Something is pushing them
To the side of their own lives.

PHILIP LARKIN


# Paternal Instruction

Children, I am training you now
to carry out the only favour
I will ever ask you. Children,
I am working for the day when
all the slaps and shouts are
cancelled out. Children, obey me.

144

I don't know for sure when
I will expect you to perform
this service. Let's say I'll
live for three score years and ten
and am exactly half way there.

So this is, in fact, a semi-anniversary;
the point at which your lesson
should begin. Andrea, say after me:
'In my teenage days I hated him,
but later saw a core of good intent.
At all events, I remembered him:
his name was Edwin and he lived.'

Nicholas say: 'He was never
a perfect father: too authoritarian;
liable to shout loudly and retire
to a quiet corner with a book.
I remember the look of him:
his name was Edwin and he lived.'

I am trusting you to repeat these
things, daily, for the remainder
of your lives. And, later, to
teach your baby-sister
something similar to say.

I do not expect my discipline
to extend to the training of
your children. When you die
I will accept the end: will
open my mouth and let the crawling
kingdom enter, and give my face
leave to crumble from my head.

EDWIN BROCK

# My Grandmother

She kept an antique shop—or it kept her.
Among Apostle spoons and Bristol glass,
The faded silks, the heavy furniture,
She watched her own reflection in the brass
Salvers and silver bowls, as if to prove
Polish was all, there was no need of love.

And I remember how I once refused
To go out with her, since I was afraid.
It was perhaps a wish not to be used
Like antique objects. Though she never said
That she was hurt, I still could feel the guilt
Of that refusal, guessing how she felt.

Later, too frail to keep a shop, she put
All her best things in one long narrow room.
The place smelt old, of things too long kept shut,
The smell of absences where shadows come
That can't be polished. There was nothing then
To give her own reflection back again.

And when she died I felt no grief at all,
Only the guilt of what I once refused.
I walked into her room among the tall
Sideboards and cupboards—things she never used
But needed: and no finger-marks were there,
Only the new dust falling through the air.

ELIZABETH JENNINGS

# Heredity

I am the family face;
Flesh perishes, I live on,
Projecting trait and trace
Through time to times anon,
And leaping from place to place
Over oblivion.

The years-heired feature that can
In curve and voice and eye
Despise the human span
Of durance—that is I;
The eternal thing in man,
That heeds no call to die.

THOMAS HARDY

 ★ **Parents and Children.** In one of his plays Oscar Wilde wrote, 'Children begin by loving their parents; after a time they judge them; rarely, if ever, do they forgive them'. *In groups*, talk about your experiences of the relationships between parents and children. Then, still in groups, prepare a reading of *Paternal Instruction* (p. 144), sharing the lines among the three characters. Individuals may be able to invent a short sequel which includes in the dialogue either what you might say to your parents or they to you.

* **Keywords.** The first three poems in this section (pp. 135–137) and the photograph of a sculpture by Henry Moore all feature a mother or father and very young children. Read through the poems to yourself and hear them spoken aloud. Then make a list of the lines, images or phrases about babies or toddlers that appeal you in these poems—'Your moth-breath flickers . . .'; '"A wolf dreamed me"' and so on. Use one or more of the ideas from your phrase collection as the 'starter' for a short poem of your own.

  Look at the Henry Moore sculpture and invent phrases as captions to describe the qualities you see—balance, confidence, poise . . .

* **Reading 'log'.** *The Almond Tree* (pp. 138–141) is a long poem in eight sections. Log your own responses to it as you read. You could either read it quietly to yourself or alternate the reading with a partner. Either way, pause after each section and jot down quickly your responses (feelings, ideas, mental pictures, expectations, associations—whatever goes through your head) so that you build up your own commentary on the poem alongside your reading.

  Afterwards, hear the poem read aloud and then discuss your responses with others in the class.

* **Generation Gap.** You may be aware of 'parents' jargon' when your mother or father is talking you. How often have you been made to feel that:
  —they are 'just trying to bring you up properly'?
  —you need 'a bit more discipline'?
  —you don't 'work hard enough'?
  —you 'shouldn't go around with *that* gang'?
  —'It wasn't like this when I was young'?
  —'When I was your age we were never allowed . . .'?
  Often the friction between the generations is caught in such phrases.

  List several of the phrases that often crop up in conversations with your mother or father. Write them down as quotations on one half of a page and alongside each one record the thoughts and feelings and unspoken comments you usually have on such occasions. Working in pairs on these notes, develop a short performance piece for two voices, one speaking the phrases, the other the private thoughts.

# Work

## Song of the Wagondriver

My first love was the ten-ton truck
they gave me when I started,
and though she played the bitch with me
I grieved when we were parted.

Since then I've had a dozen more,
the wound was quick to heal,
and now it's easier to say
I'm married to my wheel.

I've trunked it north, I've trunked it south,
on wagons good and bad,
but none were ever really like
the first I ever had.

The life is hard, the hours are long,
sometimes I cease to feel,
but I go on, for it seems to me
I'm married to my wheel.

Often I think of my home and kids,
out on the road at night,
and think of taking a local job
provided the money's right.

Two nights a week I see my wife,
and eat a decent meal,
but otherwise, for all my life,
I'm married to my wheel.

B. S. JOHNSON

# Toads

Why should I let the toad *work*
   Squat on my life?
Can't I use my wit as a pitchfork
   And drive the brute off?

Six days of the week it soils
   With its sickening poison—
Just for paying a few bills!
   That's out of proportion.

Lots of folk live on their wits:
   Lecturers, lispers,
Losels, loblolly-men, louts—
   They don't end as paupers;

Lots of folk live up lanes
   With fires in a bucket,
Eat windfalls and tinned sardines—
   They seem to like it.

Their nippers have got bare feet,
   Their unspeakable wives
Are skinny as whippets—and yet
   No one actually *starves*.

Ah, were I courageous enough
   To shout, *Stuff your pension!*
But I know, all too well, that's the stuff
   That dreams are made on:

For something sufficiently toad-like
   Squats in me too;
Its hunkers are heavy as hard luck,
   And cold as snow,

And will never allow me to blarney
   My way to getting
The fame and the girl and the money
   All at one sitting.

I don't say, one bodies the other
    One's spiritual truth;
But I do say it's hard to lose either,
    When you have both.

PHILIP LARKIN

# Work

There is no point in work
unless it absorbs you
like an absorbing game.

If it doesn't absorb you
if it's never any fun,
don't do it.

When a man goes out into his work
he is alive like a tree in spring,
he is living, not merely working.

D. H. LAWRENCE

# Cultivators

We,
who work with earth and steel
and feel winter frozen in our hands
where fields are looms,
weave the patterns of crops;
damp loam flows like silk
through shuttling metal.

And our hills,
with their wild uncurbable wills
may be hard to till
but are easy to love,
steep work weakens the tractor
but strengthens the heart.

SUSAN TAYLOR

# Stripping Walls

I have been practical as paint today, wholesome as bread—
I have stripped walls. I rose early and felt clean-limbed
And steady-eyed and said 'Today I will strip those walls.'
I have not been chewing my nails and gazing through windows
And grovelling for a subject or happiness. There was the subject.
Simple and tall. And when the baker called he was civil
And looking at me with some respect he said
'I see you're stripping walls'—I could see he liked me.
And when I opened the door to the greengrocer, I glinted my
    eyes
And leaned nonchalantly and poked some tomatoes and said as
    an aside
'I'm stripping walls today,' 'Are you?' he asked, interested, and I
    said
'Yes, just stripping those walls.' I could feel my forearms
    thicken, grow
Hairy, and when the laundry arrived I met it with rolled sleeves.
'Stripping walls?' he asked. 'Yeah,' I said, as if it were
    unimportant,
'Stripping walls. You know.' He nodded and smiled as if he
    knew.
And with a step like a spring before the meal I strode
Down to the pub and leaned and sipped ale and heard them talk
How one had cleared land that morning, another chopped
    wood.
When an eye caught mine I winked and flipped my head. 'I've
    been
Stripping walls,' I said. 'Have you?' 'Yeah, you know, just
    stripping.'
They nodded. 'Can be tricky,' one mumbled. I nodded. 'It can be
    that.'
'Plaster,' another said. 'Holes,' I said. 'Workmanship,' said
    another
And shook his head. 'Yeah, have a drink,' I said.
And whistled through the afternoon, and stood once or twice
At the door-jamb, the stripper dangling from my fingers.
'Stripping?' asked passing neighbours. I nodded and they went
    on happy—
They were happy that I was stripping walls. It meant a lot.

When it grew dark, I went out for the freshness,
   'Hey!' I called up,
'I've been stripping walls!' 'Just fancy that!' answered the moon
   with
A long pale face like Hopkins. 'Hey fellers!' he called to the stars,
'This little hairy runt has been stripping walls!' 'Bully for him,'
   chimed
The Pole star, remote and cool as Virgil, 'He's a good, good lad.'
I crept to the kitchen, pursued by celestial laughter
'You've done well today,' she said. 'Shall we paint tomorrow?'
'Ah, shut up!' I said, and started hacking my nails.

BRIAN JONES

# Mending Wall

Something there is that doesn't love a wall,
That sends the frozen-ground-swell under it,
And spills the upper boulders in the sun;
And makes gaps even two can pass abreast.
The work of hunters is another thing:
I have come after them and made repair
Where they have left not one stone on a stone,
But they would rather have the rabbit out of hiding,
To please the yelping dogs. The gaps I mean,
No one has seen them made or heard them made,
But at spring mending-time we find them there.

I let my neighbour know beyond the hill;
And on a day we meet to walk the line
And set the wall between us once again.
We keep the wall between us as we go.
To each the boulders that have fallen to each.
And some are loaves and some so nearly balls
We have to use a spell to make them balance:
'Stay where you are until our backs are turned!'
We wear our fingers rough with handling them.
Oh, just another kind of outdoor game,
One on a side. It comes to little more:
There where it is we do not need the wall:
He is all pine and I am apple orchard.
My apple trees will never get across
And eat the cones under his pines, I tell him.
He only says, 'Good fences make good neighbours.'
Spring is the mischief in me, and I wonder
If I could put a notion in his head:
'Why do they make good neighbours? Isn't it
Where there are cows? But here there are no cows.
Before I built a wall I'd ask to know
What I was walling in or walling out,
And to whom I was like to give offence.
Something there is that doesn't love a wall,
That wants it down'. I could say 'Elves' to him,
But it's not elves exactly, and I'd rather
He said it for himself. I see him there
Bringing a stone grasped firmly by the top
In each hand, like an old-stone savage armed.
He moves in darkness as it seems to me,
Not of woods only and the shade of trees.
He will not go behind his father's saying,
And he likes having thought of it so well
He says again, 'Good fences make good neighbours.'

ROBERT FROST

# Common Sense

An agricultural labourer, who has
A wife and four children, receives 20s a week
¾ buys food, and the members of the family
Have three meals a day.
How much is that per person per meal?
        *—From Pitman's Common Sense Arithmetic, 1917*

A gardener, paid 24s a week, is
Fined ⅓ if he comes to work late.
At the end of 26 weeks, he receives
£30.5.3. How
Often was he late?
        *—From Pitman's Common Sense Arithmetic, 1917*

A milk dealer buys milk at 3d a quart. He
Dilutes it with 3% water and sells
124 gallons of the mixture at
4d per quart. How much of his profit is made by
Adulterating the milk?
        *—From Pitman's Common Sense Arithmetic, 1917*

The table printed below gives the number
Of paupers in the United Kingdom, and
The total cost of poor relief.
Find the average number
Of paupers per ten thousand people.
        *—From Pitman's Common Sense Arithmetic, 1917*

An army had to march to the relief of
A besieged town, 500 miles away, which
Had telegraphed that it could hold out for 18 days.
The army made forced marches at the rate of 18
Miles a day. Would it be there in time?
        *—From Pitman's Common Sense Arithmetic, 1917*

Out of an army of 28,000 men,
15% were
Killed, 25% were
Wounded. Calculate
how many men there were left to fight.
    —*From Pitman's Common Sense Arithmetic, 1917*

These sums are offered to
That host of young people in our Elementary Schools,
   who
Are so ardently desirous of setting
Foot upon the first rung of the
Educational ladder . . .
    —*From Pitman's Common Sense Arithmetic, 1917*

ALAN BROWNJOHN

# Woman Work

I've got the children to tend
The clothes to mend
The floor to mop
The food to shop
Then the chicken to fry
The baby to dry
I got company to feed
The garden to weed
I've got the shirts to press
The tots to dress
The cane to be cut
I gotta clean up this hut
Then see about the sick
And the cotton to pick.

Shine on me, sunshine
Rain on me, rain
Fall softly, dewdrops
And cool my brow again.

Storm, blow me from here
With your fiercest wind
Let me float across the sky
'Til I can rest again.

Fall gently, snowflakes
Cover me with white
Cold icy kisses and
Let me rest tonight.

Sun, rain, curving sky
Mountain, oceans, leaf and stone
Star shine, moon glow
You're all that I can call my own.

MAYA ANGELOU

# Waterpot

The daily going out
and coming in
always being hurried
along
like like . . . cattle

In the evenings
returning from the fields
she tried hard to walk
like a woman

she tried very hard
pulling herself erect
with every three or four
steps
pulling herself together
holding herself like
royal cane

And the overseer
hurrying them along
in the quickening darkness

And the overseer sneering
them along in the quickening
darkness
sneered at the pathetic
the pathetic display
of dignity

O but look
there's a waterpot growing
from her head

GRACE NICHOLS

# I'm Gonna Be An Engineer

**Easily**

When I was a lit - tle girl I wished I was a boy, I

tagged a - long be-hind the gang and wore my cor-dur-oys,

Eve-ry-bod-y said I on - ly did it to an-noy, But I was

gon - na be an en - gi - neer.

Mom - ma told me 'Can't you be a la - dy? Your

du - ty is to make me the moth-er of a pearl.

Wait un-til you're old - er, dear, and may - be

You'll be glad that you're a girl.'

*[This part only after verses 1,3,6 and 7]*

Dain - ty as a dres - den sta - tue,

Gen - tle as a jer - sey cow; Smooth as silk, Gives

cream - y milk: Learn to coo, Learn to moo,

That's what it takes to be a lad - y now.

2. When I went to school I learned to write and how to read,
   Some history, geography and home economy,
   And typing is a skill that every girl is sure to need
   To while away the extra time until the time to breed.
   And then they had to nerve to say, 'What would you like to
       be?'
   I says 'I'm gonna be an engineer!'

   No, you only need to learn to be a lady,
   The duty isn't yours, for to try and run the world,
   An engineer could never have a baby,
   Remember, dear, that you're a girl.

3. So I become a typist and I study on the sly,
   Working out the day and night so I can qualify,
   And every time the boss come in he pinched me on the thigh,
   Says, 'I've never had an engineer!'

   You owe it to the job to be a lady,
   It's the duty of the staff for to give the boss a whirl,
   The wages that you get are crummy, maybe,
   But it's all you get cos you're a girl.

   > *She's smart (for a woman)*
   > *I wonder how she got that way?*
   > *You get no choice,*
   > *You get no voice,*
   > *Just stay mum,*
   > *Pretend you're dumb,*
   > *That's how you come to be a lady today.*

4. Then Jimmy come along and we set up a conjugation,
   We were busy every night with loving recreation,
   I spent my days at work so he could get his education
   And now he's an engineer!

   He says, 'I know you'll always be a lady
   It's the duty of my darling to love me all her life.
   Could an engineer look after or obey me?
   Remember, dear, that you're my wife!'

5. As soon as Jimmy got a job I studied hard again,
   Then, busy at me turret-lathe a year or so, and then
   The morning that the twins were born, Jimmy says to them,
   'Kids, your mother was an engineer.'

   You owe it to the kids to be a lady,
   Dainty as a dish-rag, faithful as a chow,
   Stay at home, you've got to mind the baby
   Remember you're a mother now.

6. Every time I turn around there's something else to do,
   Cook a meal or mend a sock or sweep a floor or two,
   I listen in to Jimmy Young, it makes me want to spew,
   I was gonna be an engineer.

   I really wish that I could be a lady,
   I could do the lovely things that a lady's s'posed to do,
   I wouldn't mind if only they would pay me.
   And I could be a person too.

   *What price—for a woman?*
   *You can buy her for a ring of gold;*
   *To love and obey*
   *(Without any pay)*
   *You get a cook or a nurse,*
   *For better or worse,*
   *You don't need a purse when a lady is sold.*

7. But now that times are harder, and my Jimmy's got the sack,
   I went down to Vickers, they were glad to have me back,
   I'm a third-class citizen, my wages tell me that,
   But I'm a first-class engineer,

   The boss he says, 'I pay you as a lady,
   You only got the job cos I can't afford a man.
   With you I keep the profits high as may be,
   You're just a cheaper pair of hands.'

   *You've got one fault: you're a woman,*
   *You're not worth the equal pay,*
   *A bitch or a tart,*
   *You're nothing but heart,*
   *Shallow and vain,*
   *You got no brain,*
   *Go down the drain like a lady today.*

8. I listened to my mother and I joined a typing pool,
   I listened to my lover and I sent him through his school,
   If I listen to the boss, I'm just a bloody fool,
   And an underpaid engineer.

   I've been a sucker ever since I was a baby,
   As a daughter, as a wife, as a mother and a dear,
   But I'll fight them as a woman, not a lady,
   I'll fight them as an engineer.

PEGGY SEEGER

# Engineers' Corner

Why isn't there an Engineers' Corner in Westminster
Abbey? In Britain we've always made more fuss of a
ballad than a blueprint . . . How many schoolchildren
dream of becoming great engineers?

*Advertisement placed in* The Times *by the*
*Engineering Council*

We make more fuss of ballads than the blueprints—
That's why so many poets end up rich,
While engineers scrape by in cheerless garrets.
Who needs a bridge or dam? Who needs a ditch?

Whereas the person who can write a sonnet
Has got it made. It's always been the way,
For everybody knows that we need poems
And everybody reads them every day.

Yes, life is hard if you choose engineering—
You're sure to need another job as well;
You'll have to plan your projects in the evenings
Instead of going out. It must be hell.

While well-heeled poets ride around in Daimlers,
You'll burn the midnight oil to earn a crust,
With no hope of a statue in the Abbey,
With no hope, even, of a modest bust.

No wonder small boys dream of writing couplets
And spurn the bike, the lorry and the train.
There's far too much encouragement for poets—
That's why this country's going down the drain.

WENDY COPE

# Toads Revisited

Walking around in the park
Should feel better than work:
The lake, the sunshine,
The grass to lie on,

Blurred playground noises
Beyond black-stockinged nurses—
Not a bad place to be.
Yet it doesn't suit me,

Being one of the men
You meet of an afternoon:
Palsied old step-takers,
Hare-eyed clerks with the jitters,

Waxed-fleshed out-patients
Still vague from accidents,
And characters in long coats
Deep in the litter-baskets—

All dodging the toad work
By being stupid or weak.
Think of being them!
Hearing the hours chime,

Watching the bread delivered,
The sun by clouds covered,
The children going home;
Think of being them,

Turning over their failures
By some bed of lobelias,
Nowhere to go but indoors,
No friends but empty chairs—

No, give me my in-tray,
My loaf-haired secretary,
My shall-I-keep-the-call-in-Sir:
What else can I answer,

When the lights come on at four
At the end of another year?
Give me your arm, old toad;
Help me down Cemetery Road.

PHILIP LARKIN

 ★ **Performances.** Pairs or groups rehearse and perform the
following poems, live or taped.
—*Song of the Wagondriver* (p. 149) is a modern work song. It
needs someone to invent a melody line for the verses before
performance with guitar accompaniment.
—*Stripping Walls* (p. 153) is best spoken in the self-satisfied voice
of someone who feels pleased about his D.I.Y. work, but with
the odd bits of dialogue from the baker, the grocer, etc. thrown
in by different voices. A group of four or five could rehearse a
performance.
—*Woman Work* (p. 158) is perhaps best presented on tape.
Notice how the pace slows down after the first section. Perhaps
you could suggest the bustle of these opening lines by 'over-
laying' one line with the rest, using several voices; then use single
voices for the short, later sections. Rehearse the reading various
ways before taping the version you prefer.
—*I'm Gonna Be An Engineer* (p. 160) needs someone to sing the
verses with guitar accompaniment. There's room for other voices
in the three italicised verses.

* **Work Now.** In pairs, or groups of three or four, talk about the types of non-school work that you do at present. You may well do household chores or weekend jobs to earn extra cash. Either can lead to a piece of writing. After your discussion, try one of these ideas;

—From time to time everyone becomes involved in work around the home—decorating, car or motor-bike maintenance, gardening and so on. Some of these jobs are enjoyable as hobbies, others are just duties which you may have been pressured into by your parents. There may be one task which you feel something about in one or other of these ways. Describe it carefully and try to record your feelings for it.

—If you have a part-time job—perhaps doing a newspaper round, or working in a shop, or being a delivery boy—you may feel you could write about your work. Don't forget that it is often the tiny details that you know about through first-hand experience that make for a vivid picture.

* **Found Poem: '(Un)Employment'.** A 'found poem' is one which you discover embedded in a book, a newspaper, an advert, anywhere and, through selecting and arranging the words, you make your own statement.

*Common Sense* (p. 156) is an example of what one writer found in an old maths textbook, arranged so that it makes a point about schoolwork and the purpose of education.

Newspapers and magazines have plenty to say about unemployment, job prospects for school-leavers, training schemes and so on. You, too, will have your own feelings and ideas about entering the job market.

In pairs, read and discuss Alan Brownjohn's 'found poem' and then use the same technique on the theme of '(Un)Employment'. Cut out short articles, extracts and comments on this theme and, when you have a collection of several items, edit and arrange them to make a statement about work—or the lack of it.

# Creatures

## Humming-Bird

I can imagine, in some otherworld
Primeval-dumb, far back
In that most awful stillness, that only gasped and hummed,
Humming-birds raced down the avenues.

Before anything had a soul,
While life was a heave of Matter, half inanimate,
This little bit chipped off in brilliance
And went whizzing through the slow, vast, succulent stems.

I believe there were no flowers, then
In the world where the humming-bird flashed ahead of creation.
I believe he pierced the slow vegetable veins with his long beak.

Probably he was big
As mosses, and little lizards, they say were once big.
Probably he was a jabbing, terrifying monster.

We look at him through the wrong end of the long telescope of
    Time,
Luckily for us.

D. H. LAWRENCE

169

# The Dalliance of the Eagles

Skirting the river road, (my forenoon walk, my rest,)
Skyward in air a sudden muffled sound, the dalliance of the
   eagles,
The rushing amorous contact high in space together,
The clinching interlocking claws, a living, fierce, gyrating wheel,
Four beating wings, two beaks, a swirling mass tight grappling,
In tumbling turning clustered loops, straight downward falling,
Till o'er the river pois'd, the twain yet one, a moment's lull,
A motionless still balance in the air, then parting, talons loosing,
Upward again on slow-firm pinions slanting, their separate
   diverse flight,
She hers, he his, pursuing.

WALT WHITMAN

# The Wild Swans at Coole

The trees are in their autumn beauty,
The woodland paths are dry,
Under the October twilight the water
Mirrors a still sky;
Upon the brimming water among the stones
Are nine-and-fifty swans.

The nineteenth autumn has come upon me
Since I first made my count;
I saw, before I had well finished,
All suddenly mount
And scatter wheeling in great broken rings
Upon their clamorous wings.

I have looked upon those brilliant creatures,
And now my heart is sore.
All's changed since I, hearing at twilight,
The first time on this shore,
The bell-beat of their wings above my head,
Trod with a lighter tread.

Unwearied still, lover by lover,
They paddle in the cold
Companionable streams or climb the air;
Their hearts have not grown old;
Passion or conquest, wander where they will,
Attend upon them still.

But now they drift upon the still water,
Mysterious, beautiful;
Among what rushes will they build,
By what lake's edge or pool
Delight men's eyes when I awake some day
To find they have flown away?

W. B. YEATS

# Vulture

On ragged black sails
he soars hovering over
everything and death;
a blight in the eye
of the stunning sun

An acquisitive droop
of beak, head and neck
dangles, dully angling,
a sentient pendulum
next to his keeled chest.

His eyes peer, piously
bloodless and hooded,
far-sighted, blighting
grasses, trees, hill-passes,
stones, streams, bones—ah, bones—

with the tacky slack
of flesh adherent.
A slow ritual fold
of candid devil's palms
in blasphemous prayer—

the still wings sweep closed—
the hyaena of skies
plummets from the pulpit
of a tall boredom,
swallowing as he falls.

He brakes lazily
before his back breaks
to settle on two
creaky final wing-beats
flinging twin dust-winds.

He squats once fearfully.
Flushed with unhealthy plush
and pregustatory
satisfaction, head back,
he jumps lumpishly up.

Slack neck with the pecked
skin thinly shaking, he
sidles aside then stumps
his deliberate banker's
gait to the stinking meal.

DOUGLAS LIVINGSTONE

# Snake

A snake came to my water-trough
On a hot, hot day, and I in pyjamas for the heat,
To drink there.

In the deep, strange-scented shade of the great dark carob-tree
I came down the steps with my pitcher
And must wait, must stand and wait, for there he was at the
    trough before me.

He reached down from a fissure in the earth-wall in the gloom
And trailed his yellow-brown slackness soft-bellied down, over
    the edge of the stone trough
And rested his throat upon the stone bottom,
And where the water had dripped from the tap, in a small
    clearness,
He sipped with his straight mouth,
Softly drank through his straight gums, into his slack long body,
Silently.

Someone was before me at my water-trough,
And I, like a second comer, waiting.

He lifted his head from his drinking, as cattle do,
And looked at me vaguely, as drinking cattle do,
And flickered his two-forked tongue from his lips, and mused a
    moment,
And stooped and drank a little more,
Being earth-brown, earth-golden from the burning bowels of the
    earth
On the day of Sicilian July, with Etna smoking.

The voice of my education said to me
He must be killed,
For in Sicily the black, black snakes are innocent, the gold are
    venomous.
And voices in me said, If you were a man
You would take a stick and break him now, and finish him off.

But must I confess how I liked him,
How glad I was that he had come like a guest in quiet, to drink at
    my water-trough
And depart peaceful, pacified, and thankless,
Into the burning bowels of this earth?

Was it cowardice, that I dared not kill him?
Was it perversity, that I longed to talk to him?
Was it humility, to feel so honoured?
I felt so honoured.

And yet those voices:
*If you were not afraid, you would kill him!*

And truly I was afraid, I was most afraid,
But even so, honoured still more
That he should seek my hospitality
From out the dark door of the secret earth.

He drank enough
And lifted his head, dreamily, as one who has drunken,
And flickered his tongue like a forked night on the air, so black;
Seeming to lick his lips,
And looked around like a god, unseeing, into the air,
And slowly turned his head,
And slowly, very slowly, as if thrice adream,

Proceeded to draw his slow length curving round
And climb again the broken bank of my wall-face.

And as he put his head into that dreadful hole,
And as he slowly drew up, snake-easing his shoulders, and
    entered farther,
A sort of horror, a sort of protest against his withdrawing into
    that horrid black hole,
Deliberately going into the blackness, and slowly drawing
    himself after,
Overcame me now his back was turned.

I looked round, I put down my pitcher,
I picked up a clumsy log
And threw it at the water-trough with a clatter.

I think it did not hit him,
But suddenly that part of him that was left behind convulsed in
    undignified haste,
Writhed like lightning, and was gone
Into the black hole, the earth-lipped fissure in the wall-front,
At which, in the intense still noon, I stared with fascination.

And immediately I regretted it.
I thought how paltry, how vulgar, what a mean act!
I despised myself and the voices of my accursed human
    education.

And I thought of the albatross,
And I wished he would come back, my snake.
For he seemed to me again like a king,
Like a king in exile, uncrowned in the underworld,
Now due to be crowned again.

And so, I missed my chance with one of the lords
Of life.
And I have something to expiate;
A pettiness.

                                                    D. H. LAWRENCE

# Medallion

By the gate with star and moon
Worked into the peeled orange wood
The bronze snake lay in the sun

Inert as a shoelace; dead
But pliable still, his jaw
Unhinged and his grin crooked,

Tongue a rose-coloured arrow.
Over my hand I hung him.
His little vermilion eye

Ignited with a glassed flame
As I turned him in the light;
When I split a rock one time

The garnet bits burned like that.
Dust dulled his back to ochre
The way sun ruins a trout.

Yet his belly kept its fire
Going under the chainmail,
The old jewels smouldering there

In each opaque belly-scale:
Sunset looked at through milk glass.
And I saw white maggots coil

Thin as pins in the dark bruise
Where his innards bulged as if
He were digesting a mouse.

Knifelike, he was chaste enough,
Pure death's-metal. The yardman's
Flung brick perfected his laugh.

SYLVIA PLATH

# Second Glance at a Jaguar

Skinfull of bowls, he bowls them,
The hip going in and out of joint, dropping the spine
With the urgency of his hurry
Like a cat going along under thrown stones, under cover,
Glancing sideways, running
Under his spine. A terrible, stump-legged waddle
Like a thick Aztec disembatoweller,
Club-swinging, trying to grind some square
Socket between his hind legs round,
Carrying his head like a brazier of spilling embers,
And the black bit of his mouth, he takes it
Between his back teeth, he has to wear his skin out,
He swipes a lap at the water-trough as he turns,
Swivelling the ball of his heel on the polished spot,
Showing his belly like a butterfly,
At every stride he has to turn a corner
In himself and correct it. His head
Is like the worn down stump of another whole jaguar,
His body is just the engine shoving it forward,
Lifting the air up and shoving on under,
The weight of his fangs hanging the mouth open,
Bottom jaw combing the ground. A gorged look,
Gangster, club-tail lumped along behind gracelessly,
He's wearing himself to heavy ovals,
Muttering some mantrah, some drum-song of murder
To keep his rage brightening, making his skin
Intolerable, spurred by the rosettes, the cain-brands,
Wearing the spots off from the inside,
Rounding some revenge. Going like a prayer-wheel,
The head dragging forward, the body keeping up,
The hind legs lagging. He coils, he flourishes
The blackjack tail as if looking for a target,
Hurrying through the underworld, soundless.

TED HUGHES

177

# The Horses

I climbed through woods in the hour-before-dawn dark.
Evil air, a frost-making stillness,

Not a leaf, not a bird,—
A world cast in frost. I came out above the wood

Where my breath left tortuous statues in the iron light.
But the valleys were draining the darkness

Till the moorline—blackening dregs of the brightening grey—
Halved the sky ahead. And I saw the horses:

Huge in the dense grey—ten together—
Megalith-still. They breathed, making no move,

With draped manes and tilted hind-hooves,
Making no sound.

I passed: not one snorted or jerked its head.
Grey silent fragments

Of a grey silent world.

I listened in emptiness on the moor-ridge.
The curlew's tear turned its edge on the silence.

Slowly detail leafed from the darkness. Then the sun
Orange, red, red erupted

Silently, and splitting to its core tore and flung cloud,
Shook the gulf open, showed blue,

And the big planets hanging—.
I turned

Stumbling in the fever of a dream, down towards
The dark woods, from the kindling tops,

And came to the horses.
                                    There, still they stood,

But now steaming and glistening under the flow of light,

Their draped stone manes, their tilted hind-hooves
Stirring under a thaw while all around them

The frost showed its fires. But still they made no sound.
Not one snorted or stamped

Their hung heads patient as the horizons,
High over valleys, in the red levelling rays—

In din of the crowded streets, going among the years, the faces,
May I still meet my memory in so lonely a place

Between the streams and the red clouds, hearing curlews,
Hearing the horizons endure.

TED HUGHES

# Bags of Meat

'Here's a fine bag of meat,'
Said the master-auctioneer,
As the timid, quivering steer,
Starting a couple of feet
At the prod of a drover's stick,
And trotting lightly and quick,
A ticket stuck on his rump,
Enters with a bewildered jump.

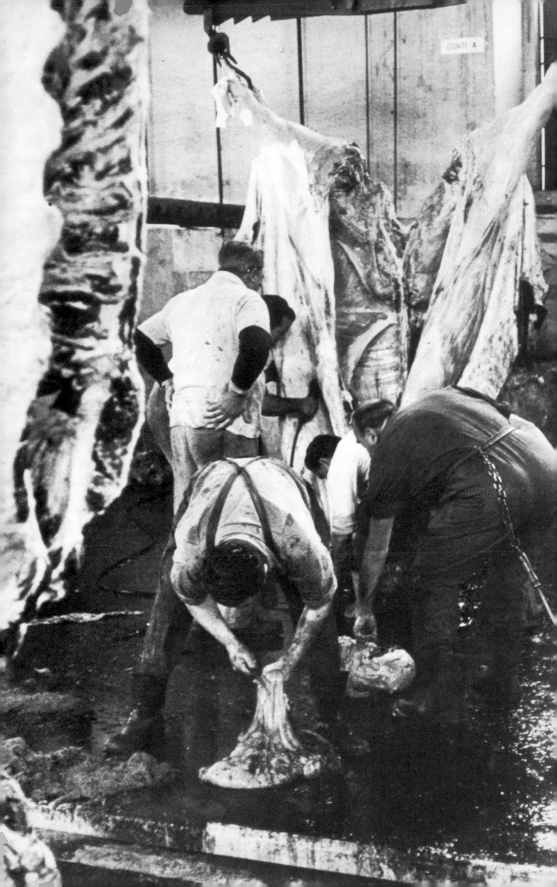

'Where he's lived lately, friends,
   I'd live till lifetime ends:
   They've a whole life everyday
   Down there in the Vale, have they!
   He'd be worth the money to kill
And give away Christmas for good-will.'

   'Now here's a heifer—worth more
   Than bid, were she bone-poor;
   Yet she's round as a barrel of beer';
'She's a plum,' said the second auctioneer.

'Now this young bull—for thirty pound?
   Worth that to manure your ground!'
'Or to stand,' chimed the second one,
   'And have his picter done!'

The beast was rapped on the horns and snout
   To make him turn about.
'Well,' cried a buyer, 'another crown—
Since I've dragged here from Taunton Town!'

   'That calf, she sucked three cows,
   Which is not matched for bouse
   In the nurseries of high life
By the first-born of a nobleman's wife!'
The stick falls, meaning, 'A true tale's told,'
On the buttock of the creature sold,
   And the buyer leans over and snips
His mark on one of the animal's hips.

   Each beast, when driven in,
Looks round at the ring of bidders there
With a much-amazed reproachful stare,
   As at unnatural kin,
For bringing him to a sinister scene
So strange, unhomelike, hungry, mean;
   A butcher, to kill out of hand,
   And a farmer, to keep on the land;
One can fancy a tear runs down his face
When the butcher wins, and he's driven from the place.

THOMAS HARDY

# Trout

Hangs, a fat gun-barrel,
deep under arched bridges
or slips like butter down
the throat of the river.

From depths smooth-skinned as plums
his muzzle gets bull's eye;
picks off grass-seed and moths
that vanish, torpedoed.

Where water unravels
over gravel-beds he
is fired from the shallows
white belly reporting

flat; darts like a tracer-
bullet back between stones
and is never burnt out.
A volley of cold blood

ramrodding the current.

SEAMUS HEANEY

# Death of a Naturalist

All year the flax-dam festered in the heart
Of the townland; green and heavy headed
Flax had rotted there, weighted down by huge sods.
Daily it sweltered in the punishing sun.
Bubbles gargled delicately, bluebottles
Wove a strong gauze of sound around the smell.
There were dragon-flies, spotted butterflies,
But best of all was the warm thick slobber
Of frogspawn that grew like clotted water
In the shade of the banks. Here, every spring
I would fill jampotfuls of the jellied
Specks to range on window-sills at home,
On shelves at school, and wait and watch until
The fattening dots burst into nimble-

Swimming tadpoles. Miss Walls would tell us how
The daddy frog was called a bullfrog
And how he croaked and how the mammy frog
Laid hundreds of little eggs and this was
Frogspawn. You could tell the weather by frogs too
For they were yellow in the sun and brown
In rain.

Then one hot day when fields were rank
With cowdung in the grass the angry frogs
Invaded the flax-dam; I ducked through hedges
To a coarse croaking that I had not heard
Before. The air was thick with a bass chorus.
Right down the dam gross-bellied frogs were cocked
On sods; their loose necks pulsed like sails. Some hopped:
The slap and plop were obscene threats. Some sat
Poised like mud grenades, their blunt heads farting.
I sickened, turned, and ran. The great slime kings
Were gathered there for vengeance and I knew
That if I dipped by hand the spawn would clutch it.

SEAMUS HEANEY

 ★ **Capturing Poets.** D. H. Lawrence and Ted Hughes are two
major poets in whose work animals feature prominently. There
are two poems by each of them in this section (pp. 169, 173, 177,
178).

Find other animals poems by these writers. (Look at Ted
Hughes' *Selected Poems 1957–81*. Faber, and D. H. Lawrence's
*Selected Poems*, Penguin.)

*In groups*, select several animal poems that you like by Hughes and Lawrence and devise a short radio programme which captures the style of either or both writers and introduces their poetry to a young audience. Script a suitable introduction and linking passages, rehearse your readings, and record your programme on cassette tape.

*Individually*, try to write your own animal poem in the style of Lawrence or Hughes. Perhaps you can invent a verse each might write about the same creature.

★ **Encounter.** Hear *Snake* (p. 173) read aloud. It's probably best shared between two voices, section by section. *In groups*, talk about the main ideas of the poem and note down the places where Lawrence's thoughts and feelings change. You could present these as a flow-diagram; or as a graph with different coloured lines for 'the voices of his education' and for his instinctive feelings of admiration for the snake. Either way, show how the narrative of the poem develops.

If the poem reminds you of a significant anecdote you can tell about a creature, first, plot out the events in sequence, concentrating simply upon what happened. Then plot out the internal narrative of your own changing feelings and thoughts. Work the two in together to make your poem.

★ **Class Bestiary.** Most of the creatures in this section are caught in particular images:
—swans . . . 'scatter wheeling in great broken rings'
—eagles . . . 'clinching, interlocking claws'
—the vulture . . . 'on ragged black sails he soars'
—a snake . . . 'inert as a shoelace'
—a heifer . . . 'round as a barrel of beer'
—a trout . . . 'a fat gun-barrel'
—frogspawn is . . . 'clotted water' and frogs are . . . 'mud grenades'.

Make up your own class bestiary. All you need to start is a sheet of paper and a different animal for everyone in the class, though pictures of animals would also help. Head up each sheet with the animal's name (and picture if you have one). Write *one* short 'image association', like those above, and pass your paper on. Circulate the papers until you have collected as many images as possible. Work the ideas and images the class has given you into a list-poem or prose description of the animal. The class bestiary can then be put up for display.

184

# Poems to Compare

## A. End of the World

The world's end came as a small dot
    at the end of a sentence. Everyone died
without ado, and nobody cried
    enough to show the measure of it.

God said 'I do not love you', quite
    quietly, but with a final note;
it seemed the words caught in his throat,
    or else he stifled a yawn as the trite

phrase escaped his dust-enlivening lips.
    At least, there was no argument,
no softening tact, no lover's cant,
    but sudden vacuum, total eclipse

of sense and meaning. The world had gone
    and everything on it, except the lives
all of us had to live: the wives,
    children, clocks which ticked on,

unpaid bills, enormous power-blocks
    chock-full of arms demanding peace,
and the prayerful in a state of grace
    pouncing on bread and wine like hawks.

TONY CONNOR

## The End of the World

Quite unexpectedly as Vasserot
The armless ambidextrian was lighting
A match between his great and second toe

185

And Ralph the lion was engaged in biting
The neck of Madame Sossman while the drum
Pointed, and Teeny was about to cough
In waltz-time swinging Jocko by the thumb—
Quite unexpectedly the top blew off:

And there, there overhead, there, there, hung over
Those thousands of white faces, those dazed eyes,
There in the starless dark, the poise, the hover,
There with vast wings across the cancelled skies,
There in the sudden blackness the black pall
Of nothing, nothing, nothing—nothing at all.

ARCHIBALD McLEISH

186

# B.  Delight in Disorder

A sweet disorder in the dresse
Kindles in cloathes a wantonnesse:
A Lawne about the shoulders thrown
Into a fine distraction:
An erring Lace, which here and there
Enthralls the Crimson Stomacher:
A Cuffe neglectfull and thereby
Ribbands to flow confusedly:
A winning wave (deserving Note)
In the tempestuous petticote:
A carelesse shooe-string, in whose tye
I see a wilde civility:
Doe more bewitch me, than when Art
Is too precise in every part.

ROBERT HERRICK


# Sweet Neglect

Still to be neat, still to be drest,
As you were going to a feast:
Still to be powdered, still perfumed:
Lady, it is to be presumed.
Though art's hid causes are not found,
All is not sweet, all is not sound.

Give me a look, give me a face
That makes simplicity a grace;
Robes loosely flowing, hair as free:
Such sweet neglect more taketh me,
Than all th'adulteries of art,
That strike mine eyes, but not my heart.

BEN JONSON

## C. Early Morning Feed

The father darts out on the stairs
To listen to the keening
In the upper room, for a change of note
That signifies distress, to scotch disaster,
The kettle humming in the room behind.

He thinks, on tiptoe, ears a-strain,
The cool dawn rising like the moon:
'Must not appear and pick him up;
He mustn't think he has me springing
To his beck and call,'
The kettle rattling behind the kitchen door.

He has him springing
A-quiver on the landing—
For a distress-note, a change of key,
To gallop up the stairs to him
To take him up, light as a violin,
And stroke his back until he smiles.
He sidles in the kitchen
And pours his tea . . .

And again stands hearkening
For milk cracking the lungs.
There's a little panting,
A cough: the thumb's in: he'll sleep,
The cup of tea cooling on the kitchen table.

Can he go in now to his chair and think
Of the miracle of breath, pick up a book,
Ready at all times to take it at a run
And intervene between him and disaster,
Sipping his cold tea as the sun comes up?

He returns to bed
And feels like something, with the door ajar,
Crouched in the bracken, alert, with big eyes
For the hunter, death, disaster.

PETER REDGROVE

# The Zulu Girl

When in the sun the hot red acres smoulder,
Down where the sweating gang its labour plies,
A girl flings down her hoe, and from her shoulder
Unslings her child tormented by the flies.

She takes him to a ring of shadow pooled
By thorn-trees: purpled with the blood of ticks,
While her sharp nails, in slow caresses ruled,
Prowl through his hair with sharp electric clicks,

His sleepy mouth plugged by the heavy nipple,
Tugs like a puppy, grunting as he feeds:
Through his frail nerves her own deep langours ripple
Like a broad river sighing through its reeds.

Yet in that drowsy stream his flesh imbibes
An old unquenched unsmotherable heat—
The curbed ferocity of beaten tribes,
The sullen dignity of their defeat.

Her body looms above him like a hill
Within whose shade a village lies at rest,
Or the first cloud so terrible and still
That bears the coming harvest in its breast.

ROY CAMPBELL

# D. The Clod and the Pebble

'Love seeketh not itself to please,
Nor for itself hath any care,
But for another gives its ease,
And builds a Heaven in Hell's despair.'

So sung a little Clod of Clay,
Trodden with the cattle's feet,
But a Pebble of the brook
Warbled out these metres meet:

'Love seeketh only Self to please,
To bind another to its delight,
Joys in another's loss of ease,
And builds a Hell in Heaven's despite.'

WILLIAM BLAKE

# Love

The difficult part of love
Is being selfish enough,
Is having the blind persistence
To upset someone's existence
Just for your own sake—
What cheek it must take.

And then the unselfish side—
Who can be satisfied
Putting someone else first,
So that you come off worst?
My life is for me:
As well deny gravity.

Yet, vicious or virtuous,
Love still suits most of us;
Only the bleeder who
Can't manage either view
Is ever wholly rebuffed—
And he can get stuffed.

PHILIP LARKIN

# E.  In Oak Terrace

Old and alone, she sits at nights,
nodding before the television.
The house is quiet now. She knits,
rises to put the kettle on,

watches a cowboy's killing, reads
the local Births and Deaths, and falls
asleep at 'Growing stock-piles of war-heads'.
A world that threatens worse ills

fades. She dreams of a life spent
in the one house: suffers again
poverty, sickness, abandonment,
a child's death, a brother's brain

melting to madness. Seventy years
of common trouble; the kettle sings.
At midnight she says her silly prayers,
and takes her teeth out, and collects her night-things.

TONY CONNOR

# Love Songs in Age

She kept her songs, they took so little space,
   The covers pleased her:
One bleached from lying in a sunny place,
One marked in circles by a vase of water,
One mended, when a tidy fit had seized her,
   And coloured, by her daughter—
So they had waited, till in widowhood
She found them, looking for something else, and stood

Relearning how each frank submissive chord
   Had ushered in
Word after sprawling hyphenated word,
And the unfailing sense of being young
Spread out like a spring-woken tree, wherein
   That hidden freshness sung,
That certainty of time laid up in store
As when she played them first. But, even more,

The glare of that much-mentioned brilliance, love,
   Broke out, to show
Its bright incipience sailing above,
Still promising to solve, and satisfy,
And set unchangeably in order. So
   To pile them back, to cry,
Was hard, without lamely admitting how
It had not done so then, and could not now.

PHILIP LARKIN

# F. Holy Sonnet

Batter my heart, three person'd God; for you
As yet but knocke, breathe, shine, and seeke to mend;
That I may rise, and stand, o'erthrow mee, 'and bend
Your force, to breake, blowe, burn and make me new.
I, like an usurpt towne, to'another due,
Labour to'admit you, but Oh, to no end,
Reason your viceroy in mee, mee should defend,
But is captiv'd, and proves weake or untrue.
Yet dearely'I love you, and would be lov'd faine,
But am betroth'd unto your enemie:
Divorce mee, 'untie, or breake that knot againe,
Take mee to you, imprison mee, for I
Except you'enthrall mee, never shall be free,
Nor ever chast, except you ravish mee.

JOHN DONNE

# Thou Art Indeed Just, Lord

Thou art indeed just, Lord, if I contend
With thee; but, sir, so what I plead is just.
Why do sinners' ways prosper? and why must
Disappointment all I endeavour end?
   Wert thou my enemy, O thou my friend,
How wouldst thou worse, I wonder, than thou dost
Defeat, thwart me? Oh, the sots and thralls of lust
Do in spare hours more thrive than I that spend,
Sir, life upon thy cause. See, banks and brakes
Now, leavèd how thick! lacèd they are again
With fretty chervil, look, and fresh wind shakes
Them; birds build—but not I build; no, but strain,
Time's eunuch, and not breed one work that wakes.
Mine, O thou lord of life, send my roots rain.

GERARD MANLEY HOPKINS

# G. Pike

Pike, three inches long, perfect
Pike in all part, green tigering the gold.
Killers from the egg: the malevolent aged grin.
They dance on the surface among the flies.

Or move, stunned by their own grandeur,
Over a bed of emerald, silhouette
Of submarine delicacy and horror.
A hundred feet long in their world.

In ponds, under the heat-struck lily pads—
Gloom of their stillness:
Logged on last year's black leaves, watching upwards.
Or hung in an amber cavern of weeds

The jaws' hooked clamp and fangs
Not to be changed at this date;
A life subdued to its instrument;
The gills kneading quietly, and the pectorals.

Three we kept behind glass,
Jungled in weed: three inches, four,
And four and a half: fed fry to them—
Suddenly there were two. Finally one

With a sag belly and the grin it was born with.
And indeed they spare nobody.

Two, six pounds each, over two feet long,
High and dry and dead in the willow-herb—

One jammed past its gills down the other's gullet:
The outside eye stared: as a vice locks—
The same iron in this eye
Though its film shrank in death.

A pond I fished, fifty yards across,
Whose lilies and muscular tench
Had outlasted every visible stone
Of the monastery that planted them—

Stilled legendary depth:
It was as deep as England. It held
Pike too immense to stir, so immense and old
That past nightfall I dared not cast

But silently cast and fished
With the hair frozen on my head
For what might move, for what eye might move.
The still splashes on the dark pond.

Owls hushing the floating woods
Frail on my ear against the dream
Darkness beneath night's darkness had freed,
That rose slowly towards me, watching.

TED HUGHES

# The Pike

From shadows of rich oaks outpeer
The moss-green bastions of the weir,
Where the quick dipper forages
In elver-peopled crevices,
And a small runlet trickling down the sluice
Gossamer music tires not to unloose.

Else round the broad pool's hush
    Nothing stirs,
Unless sometime a straggling heifer crush
Through the thronged spinney where the pheasant whirs;
   Or martins in a flash
Come with wild mirth to dip their magical wings,
While in the shallow some doomed bulrush swings
At whose hid root the diver vole's teeth gnash.

And nigh this toppling reed, still as the dead
   The great pike lies, the murderous patriarch
   Watching the waterpit sheer-shelving dark,
Where through the plash his lithe bright vassals thread.

The rose-finned roach and bluish bream
And staring ruffe steal up the stream
Hard by their glutted tyrant, now
Still as a sunken bough.

He on the sandbank lies,
   Sunning himself long hours
With stony gorgon eyes:
   Westward the hot sun lowers.

Sudden the gray pike changes, and quivering poises for
      slaughter;
   Intense terror wakens around him, the shoals scud awry, but
      there chances
   A chub unsuspecting; the prowling fins quicken, in fury he
      lances;
And the miller that opens the hatch stands amazed at the whirl
      in the water.

EDMUND BLUNDEN

# H. Revelation

I remember once being shown the black bull
when a child at the farm for eggs and milk.
They called him Bob—as though perhaps
you could reduce a monster
with the charm of a friendly name.
At the threshold of his outhouse, someone
held my hand and let me peer inside.
At first, only black
and the hot reek of him. Then he was immense,
his edges merging with the darkness, just
a big bulk and a roar to be really scared of,
a trampling, and a clanking tense with the chain's jerk.
His eyes swivelled in the great wedge of his tossed head.
He roared his rage. His nostrils gaped.

And in the yard outside,
oblivious hens picked their way about.
The faint and rather festive tinkling
behind the mellow stone and hasp was all they knew
of that Black Mass, straining at his chains.
I had always half-known he existed—
this antidote and Anti-Christ his anarchy
threatening the eggs, well rounded, self-contained—
and the placidity of milk.

I ran, my pigtails thumping on my back in fear,
past the big boys in the farm lane
who pulled the wings from butterflies and
blew up frogs with straws.
Past throned hedge and harried nest,
scared of the eggs shattering—
only my small and shaking hand on the jug's rim
in case the milk should spill.

LIZ LOCHHEAD

# The Bull Moses

A hoist up and I could lean over
The upper edge of the high half-door,
My left foot ledged on the hinge, and look in at the byre's
Blaze of darkness: a sudden shut-eyed look
Backward into the head.

     Blackness is depth
Beyond star. But the warm weight of his breathing,
The ammoniac reek of his litter, the hotly-tongued
Mash of his cud, steamed against me.
Then, slowly, as onto the mind's eye—
The brow like masonry, the deep-keeled neck:
Something came up there onto the brink of the gulf,
Hadn't heard of the world, too deep in itself to be called to,
Stood in sleep. He would swing his muzzle at a fly
But the square of sky where I hung, shouting, waving,
Was nothing to him; nothing of our light
Found any reflection in him.

     Each dusk the farmer led him
Down to the pond to drink and smell the air,
And he took no pace but the farmer
Led him to take it, as if he knew nothing
Of the ages and continents of his fathers,
Shut, while he wombed, to a dark shed
And steps between his door and the duckpond;
The weight of the sun and the moon and the world hammered
To a ring of brass through his nostrils.

     He would raise
His streaming muzzle and look out over the meadows,
But the grasses whispered nothing awake, the fetch
Of the distance drew nothing to momentum
In the locked black of his powers. He came strolling gently back.
Paused neither towards the pig-pens on his right,
Nor towards the cow-byres on his left: something
Deliberate in his leisure, some beheld future
Founding in his quiet.

     I kept the door wide,
Closed it after him and pushed the bolt.     TED HUGHES

# I. Musée des Beaux Arts

About suffering they were never wrong,
The Old Masters: how well they understood
Its human position; how it takes place
While someone else is eating or opening a window or just
    walking dully along;
How, when the aged are reverently, passionately waiting
For the miraculous birth, there always must be
Children who did not specially want it to happen, skating
On a pond at the edge of the wood:
They never forgot
That even the dreadful martyrdom must run its course
Anyhow in a corner, some untidy spot
Where the dogs go on with their doggy life and the torturer's
    horse
Scratches its innocent behind on a tree.

In Brueghel's *Icarus*, for instance: how everything turns away
Quite leisurely from the disaster; the ploughman may
Have heard the splash, the forsaken cry,
But for him it was not an important failure; the sun shone
As it had to on the white legs disappearing into the green
Water; and the expensive delicate ship that must have seen
Something amazing, a boy falling out of the sky,
Had somewhere to get to and sailed calmly on.

W. H. AUDEN

# Fall of Icarus: Brueghel

Flashing through falling sunlight
A frantic leg late plunging from its strange
Communicating moment
Flutters in shadowy waves.

Close by those shattered waters—
The spray, no doubt, struck shore—
One dreamless shepherd and his old sheep dog
Define outrageous patience
Propped on staff and haunches,
Intent on nothing, backs bowed against the sea,
While the slow flocks of sheep gnaw on the grass-thin coast.
Crouched in crimson homespun an indifferent peasant
Guides his blunt plow through gravelled ground,
Cutting flat furrows hugging this hump of land.
One partridge sits immobile on its bough
Watching a Flemish fisherman pursue
Fish in the darkening bay;
Their stillness mocks rude ripples rising and circling in.

Yet that was a stunning greeting
For any old angler, peasant, or the grand ship's captain,
Though sent by a mere boy
Bewildered in the gravitational air,
Flashing his wild white arms at the impassive sea-drowned sun.

Now only coastal winds
Ruffle the partridge feathers,
Muting the soft ripping of sheep cropping,
The heavy whisper
Of furrows falling, ship cleaving,
Water lapping.

Lulled in the loose furl and hum of infamous folly,
Darkly, how silently, the cold sea suckles him.

JOSEPH LANGLAND

# Landscape with the Fall of Icarus

According to Brueghel
when Icarus fell
it was spring

a farmer was ploughing
his field
the whole pageantry

of the year was
awake tingling
near

the edge of the sea
concerned
with itself

sweating in the sun
that melted
the wings' wax

unsignificantly
off the coast
there was

a splash quite unnoticed
this was
Icarus drowning

WILLIAM CARLOS WILLIAMS

# J. Afterwards

When the Present has latched its postern behind my tremulous
     stay,
    And the May month flaps its glad green leaves like wings,
Delicate-filmed as new-spun silk, will the neighbours say,
    'He was a man who used to notice such things'?

If it be in the dusk when, like an eyelid's soundless blink,
    The dewfall-hawk[1] comes crossing the shades to alight
Upon the wind-warped upland thorn, a gazer may think,
    'To him this must have been a familiar sight.'

If I pass during some nocturnal blackness, mothy and warm,
    When the hedgehog travels furtively over the lawn,
One may say, 'He strove that such innocent creatures should
     come to no harm,
    But he could do little for them; and now he is gone.'

If, when hearing that I have been stilled at last, they stand at the
     door,
    Watching the full-starred heavens that winter sees,
Will this thought rise on those who will meet my face no more,
    'He was one who had an eye for such mysteries'?

And will any say when my bell of quittance is heard in the
     gloom,
    And a crossing breeze cuts a pause in its outrollings,
Till they rise again, as they were a new bell's boom,
    'He hears it not now, but used to notice such things'?

THOMAS HARDY

[1] barn owl

# Poem for a Dead Poet

He was a poet he was.
A proper poet.
He said things
that made you think
and said them nicely.
He saw things
that you or I
could never see
and saw them clearly.
He had a way
with language.
Images flocked around
him like birds,
St Francis, he was,
of the words. Words?
Why he could almost make 'em talk.

ROGER McGOUGH

# Acknowledgments

The editors and publishers would like to thank the following for their kind permission to reproduce copyright material:

Fleur Adcock: 'Earlswood' © Fleur Adcock 1986. Reprinted from *The Incident Book* by Fleur Adcock (1986) by permission of Oxford University Press. John Agard: 'Anancy's Thoughts on Love', by permission of the author. Maya Angelou: 'Phenomenal Woman' and 'Woman's Work' from *And Still I Rise*, Virago Press Ltd. W. H. Auden: 'As I Walked Out One Evening', 'Refugee Blues', 'The Unknown Citizen' and 'Musée des Beaux Arts' from *Collected Shorter Poems 1927–57*, reprinted by permission of Faber & Faber Ltd. Michael Baldwin: 'Death on a Live Wire' from *Death on a Live Wire and Other Poems*, Longman, by permission of the author. Edmund Blunden: 'The Pike' from *Poems of Many Years*, Collins Sons & Co. Ltd and reprinted by permission of A. D. Peters and Co. Edwin Brock: 'Five Ways to Kill a Man' from *With Love from Judas*, Scorpion Press; 'Paternal Instruction' by permission of the author. Alan Brownjohn: 'For my Son' and 'Common Sense', by permission of the author, pending publication by Century Hutchinson (1988). Roy Campbell: 'The Zulu Girl' from *Collected Poems*, Faber & Faber Ltd, by permission of the estate of Roy Campbell. William Carlos Williams: 'Landscape with the Fall of Icarus' from *Pictures from Brueghel*. Copyright © 1962 by William Carlos Williams. Reprinted by permission of New Directions Publishing Corporation. Tony Connor: 'Child Half Asleep' from *Kon in Springtime*; 'In Oak Terrace' from *Lodgers*; 'End of the World' and 'St Mark's Cheetham Hill' from *With Love Somehow*, reprinted by permission of Oxford University Press. Wendy Cope: 'Mr Strugnell' and 'Engineers' corner' from *Making Cocoa for Kingsley Amis*, reprinted by permission of Faber & Faber Ltd. e. e. cummings: 'ygUDuh' from *Complete Poems 1936–1962*, MacGibbon & Kee Ltd. Emily Dickinson: 'Because I Could Not Stop for Death' reprinted by permission of the publishers and trustees for Amherst College from Thomas H. Johnson, editor, *The Poems of Emily Dickinson*, Cambridge, Mass.; the Belknap Press of Harvard University Press, copyright 1951, 1955 by the